REAL STRENGTH

Build your resilience and bounce back from *anything*

PSYCHOLOGIES
MAGAZINE

This edition first published 2017
© 2017 Kelsey Publishing Ltd

Registered office
John Wiley and Sons Ltd, The Atrium, Southern Gate, Chichester, West Sussex, PO19 8SQ,
United Kingdom

For details of our global editorial offices, for customer services and for information about
how to apply for permission to reuse the copyright material in this book please see our
website at www.wiley.com.

Library of Congress Cataloging-in-Publication Data is available

A catalogue record for this book is available from the British Library.

ISBN 978-0-857-08669-3 (pbk)
ISBN 978-0-857-08670-9 (ebk) ISBN 978-0-857-08671-6 (ebk)

Cover design: Wiley

Set in 9.5/13pt ITC Franklin Gothic Std by Aptara Inc., New Delhi, India

Printed in Great Britain by TJ International Ltd, Padstow, Cornwall, UK

CONTENTS

FOREWORD

by Suzy Greaves, Editor, *Psychologies*

D ivorce, debt, redundancy, loss of loved ones. We wouldn't be human if we didn't struggle in the face of such ordeals. But what would it be like if we could learn the skills of not only surviving such challenges, but learning and growing because of them?

At *Psychologies*, we believe that real strength is not about powering through a crisis with a stiff upper lip. It's about using life's challenges to reset your course, for you to be able to admit vulnerability, tell the truth about how you feel and then find a way to move forward again.

Yes, when you are first faced with huge changes it is a massive shock to the system, and you can feel lost, scared, sad and confused. But real strength is about feeling all of those emotions and then finding a way to centre yourself again and respond from a place of hope and optimism versus fear. It's not about inane optimism either. You are allowed to prepare for the worst as well as hope for the best. Real strength is about finding a sense of meaning in the adversity. It can be an opportunity to look at how you are spending your time and your energy and committing to a life that is built on your values.

At *Psychologies*, we believe that each and every one of us has an innate wisdom to help choose the right path. Right now, you may not know what that path may be, but by picking up this book you have taken the first step to finding a way through the challenges you may be currently facing and building the resilience you need to create the life you want.

And we are right by your side.

Good luck!

Suzy Greaves, Editor, *Psychologies*

INTRODUCTION

There are obviously a million possible reasons why you picked up this book, but we would hazard a guess that a big part of it is because, right now, you could do with some real strength. We'd like to point out that that alone – the fact you are on the hunt for things to help yourself in your current situation – indicates you are already stronger and more resilient than you think. Being able to seek support is an important part of building strength.

'When life gives you lemons, make lemonade' or so the saying goes. And this is possibly what this book is about in a nutshell. No one can escape the lemons, after all. There are not many things we can guarantee in life but the fact we will all, at some point, come across adversity is one of them. Adversity, trauma, pain, struggles – call it what you will – upheaval happens in our lives whether we like it or not and, chances are, it's happening to you right now.

This could be subtle upheaval such as rows with loved ones and disappointments, or more serious trauma such as bereavement, getting divorced and illness. It doesn't have to be an 'event' at all; you could just feel that you are in a rut. We are all thrown a curveball once in a while but it's how we react and deal with those curveballs that makes us stronger. And crucially, how we grow from them. That's what we believe real strength is at *Psychologies* magazine – not just surviving hard times, but thriving because, and in spite of them – and this is what this book aims to help you to do.

But just as the traumas we will all experience in our lives will differ hugely, so will our perceptions of those experiences. The same can be said of what we constitute as real strength all we can say, is that 'real' is the crucial word here; because it's about what feels real and authentic to you, what makes *you* feel strong.

That's probably the most important ethos here at *Psychologies* magazine: you are an individual and what helps and inspires you when you hit a rough patch won't necessarily help the next person. That's why we'd like you to see *Real Strength* as a toolkit for unlocking and building upon *your* inner resilience; your ability, not just to bounce back from adversity, but to use it as a platform to bounce even higher. And this is perfectly within your reach. It's likely that it doesn't feel like that right now, but trust us, it is.

In fact, we're here not only to help you believe that, but to show you how it's done. Using the latest research and advice from experts in fields of wellbeing and resilience, *Real Strength* aims to help you define your own brand of resilience and to develop the skills to tap into it. We sincerely believe that if you can do that, there is greater joy and contentment waiting for you around the corner and it's very probable you will come to see this hardship you're going through as the greatest gift you were ever given.

HOW TO USE THIS BOOK

We've divided this book into three parts:

1. What Does Real Strength Mean to You?
2. What's Stopping You from Bouncing Back?
3. How Can You Build Real Strength?

In Part 1, you'll gain an overview of the interpretations – current and not so current – of real strength in our culture. We'll invite you to look at all the different ways in which we, at *Psychologies*, define it, and encourage you to decide which parts of the list chime most with you in order to curate your own definition. Or at least to decide which facets of real strength you'd like to work on the most.

In Part 2, we'll help you to understand what obstacles you might be coming up against that are stopping you from feeling and being stronger. We'll look at whether certain people are naturally more resilient than others – what skills and qualities they have that you could learn and how to learn them. Also, there's a section on 'strength robbers' – common pitfalls we fall into that chip away at our ability to be resilient.

In Part 3, we give you real techniques and actual therapies that professionals use that will help you to build strength and resilience in the most empowering and lasting way possible. We aim for these practical steps to be things you can take away with you for the rest of your life. We don't want to keep you waiting until the final part for practical help though, so throughout the book you'll find tips that you can try out in order to start feeling better and stronger right now.

THE EXPERTS INTERVIEWED FOR *REAL STRENGTH*

Liggy Webb, Consultant in Behavioural Skills

Liggy Webb is a leading author, presenter and thought leader on resilience. She has researched and developed a range of techniques and practical approaches to support both individuals and organizations to cope more effectively and successfully with the demands and challenges of life.

Some of the organizations she has worked with include the United Nations, the World Trade Organization, BBC, NHS, Macmillan Cancer Support, Sainsbury's, Ralph Lauren and Walt Disney.

Liggy is also the founding director of The Learning Architect, an international consortium of behavioural skills specialists.

She is recognized as a thought leader on resilience and is regularly asked to be a keynote speaker across private and public sectors.

Liggy's latest book *Resilience: How To Cope When Everything Around You Keeps Changing* is a practical and accessible guide for coping with change and offers advice on how to how to bounce back from challenging situations.

Dr Michael Sinclair, Consultant Counselling Psychologist

Dr Michael Sinclair is an Associate Fellow of the British Psychological Society and a Chartered Scientist registered with the Science Council. He works with individuals, couples and families who are experiencing a wide range of psychological problems, such as depression and anxiety. He also provides cutting-edge stress management training to corporate employees as well as mindfulness workshops for the public.

He is one of the founders and the Clinical Director of City Psychology Group in London. He is the consultant to several corporate occupational health departments advising on employees' mental health and wellbeing. He also provides psychological consultancy and performance coaching to senior managers working in law and finance, as well as training and supervision to other health practitioners and psychologists.

He has worked as a psychologist within schools, specialist mental health clinics and GP's surgeries and The Royal Free Hospital in London. He is particularly skilled in delivering cognitive behavioural therapy (CBT), as well as being highly experienced in Acceptance and Commitment Therapy (ACT) and other mindfulness-based approaches for behavioural change.

He has published a range of self-help books, including: *Fear and Self-Loathing in the City: A Guide To Keeping Sane In The*

Square Mile, The Little CBT Workbook: A Step By Step Guide To Gaining Control Of Your Life, Mindfulness for Busy People: Turning Frantic and Frazzled into Calm and Composed and *Working with Mindfulness: Keeping Calm and Focussed to Get the Job Done*.

His latest book is *The Little ACT Workbook, An Introduction to Acceptance and Commitment Therapy: A Mindfulness-Based Guide for Leading a Full and Meaningful Life*.

1 WHAT DOES REAL STRENGTH MEAN TO YOU?

CHAPTER 1

WHAT IS *REAL* STRENGTH?

W hat comes to mind when you think of the word 'strength'? Not the sort of strength that means you can lift weights at the gym of course, but mental and emotional strength (although you could argue that you need a degree of the latter, to do the former). You often hear people say, 'she's such a strong person' or 'he'll be alright, he's strong', but what do they mean? Chances are, everybody will mean something slightly different, and the sort of person your friend or your mum or your colleague thinks of as strong may not be the sort of person you think of.

Try it now: if you were to describe a strong person, or identify someone you already know who you think of as mentally strong, who would you choose? What qualities and traits do they possess? Perhaps you see a strong person as stoic; someone who rarely complains and seems to be able to withstand more pain and adversity than others; or perhaps it is someone who possesses military-style toughness – who seems fearless and enjoys pushing themselves to the limit. Write down the name of the person or people if you like, and a list of what makes them strong in your opinion.

This is a useful exercise for defining your notions of real strength as they are right now, but the purpose of this chapter is to hold up those current notions and examine them; if necessary, to challenge them. Because while stoicism, toughness and so on definitely have their value, we believe that *real* strength is a lot more subtle, complex and wide-reaching than that. It's certainly not as simple as the opposite of weakness. In fact, it's probably not what you think it is at all. When you discover what real strength is really about, we bet you'll realize you're already much stronger than you think.

Before we begin to help you tap into the reserves of strength you already have, and help you build more, let's explore definitions of real strength – current and more outdated. It's important to point out that this isn't THE definitive list because, as we've said, real strength is open to interpretation. Instead, see it more as an exploration of real strength. The idea, then, is that you can use this list as inspiration. You can decide which versions of strength mean the most to you. Crucially, you can decide which facets of real strength you could benefit most from working on in order to help you not just survive this bump in the road, but to come out thriving. Not just to bounce back, but to bounce higher. Because we all have reserves of strength, it's just knowing how to access them. Once you can do that, you really can triumph over adversity and find deeper joy and satisfaction in your life.

DEFINING REAL STRENGTH

1. Real strength is about resilience

When you think of the word 'strong', chances are certain synonyms come to mind: tough, robust, resilient, determined ... Of all these, resilient is probably the closest to what we mean when we talk about *real* strength. You could go so far as to say that the two words are interchangeable.

Still, there are so many ways to define strength and resilience. If we look up 'strength' in the *Oxford Dictionary*, there are no less than 18 definitions. These include:

1. Capacity for moral effort or endurance.
2. Power to sustain force without breaking or yielding.
3. Physical power.

For 'resilience' alone, there are three:

1. The action or an act of rebounding or springing back.
2. Elasticity.
3. The ability to recover readily from, or resist being affected by, a setback, an illness.

If we were to take all these descriptions and turn them into a three-word description, we could say that resilience/real strength is 'thriving despite adversity'. That's about it in a nutshell. But let's delve deeper ...

The word resilience[1] first came into use in the 1970s. Emmy Werner was one of the first scientists to use the word resilience to describe a group of children from Kauai, Hawaii, who despite growing up in poverty with alcoholic and mentally-ill parents, still thrived as adults (whereas another group exhibited destructive behaviours). Resilience soon became used as a term in psychology, and many years later, in 2007, was defined as: 'The capacity to withstand traumatic situations and the ability to use trauma as the start of something new.'

Then, at the beginning of the 21st century, the business world picked up on the concept of resilience and came up with something called Resilience Engineering: 'the ability to reinvent business models and strategies as, and if, circumstances change'.

Now, you may wonder what on earth business definitions of resilience have to do with the human sort and, more importantly, real strength, but we think it's rather a lot. In fact, if we analyse what Resilience Engineering is all about it helps us reach a much more sophisticated understanding of what we mean when we talk about *real* strength. After all, if they can engineer resilience for businesses, then surely we can do it for ourselves. The Resilience Engineering website (www.resilience-engineering-association.org) defines a resilient individual (or system) as one that can 'sustain required operations under both expected and unexpected conditions' as well as being able to 'do what's required under a variety of conditions, rather than just the ability to recover from threats and stresses'.

---

[1] To describe human beings at least, as opposed to types of timber, which is the only way the word was used for a long time!

OK, the language might be slightly dry, but both these definitions make a really important point and distinction between, say, toughness or robustness and *real* strength. Most people can bounce back, after all, from a one-off disappointment or failure, such as not getting a job they go for, or even quite a big change in circumstances – such as breaking up with a long-term partner. However, it's people who can continually adjust themselves, and remain true to their values when faced with sustained and unexpected changes, that are truly strong.

> **"The best thing anyone described [resilience] to me as, was 'emotional sun-screen'; it's not covering yourself with a protective shield but it is about creating a protective layer."**
>
> Liggy Webb, consultant in behavioural skills and author of *Resilience*

2. Real strength is not about staying safe or self-protection

Being truly strong is *not* necessarily about looking at a challenge, working out the probability of failure and then deciding whether or not to attempt it. Instead it's about creating flexible techniques that are robust, and knowing your strengths and weaknesses in order to tackle that challenge head on.

Real strength, then, is not about keeping yourself 'safe' (more of this in a minute), but knowing how to tackle the situation when you're not. It's also about being able to respond effectively to both disturbance *and* opportunity (in a business context we can see how this is vital, but it works for human beings too). Given the unknowns they both present, you're likely to feel anything but safe in either situation, but real strength is knowing how to dive in anyway.

3. Real strength is not about avoiding pain, but embracing it

We already talked in the introduction about the fact that pain and trauma are an unavoidable part of life, and that it's how you deal with them that separates the resilient from the not-so resilient. We will be looking at strategies to tackle adversity (good and bad) in more detail throughout the book, but for now, it's perhaps helpful to remember that as human beings:

> 66 **Often our attempts to get rid of pain can add extra suffering and can be time consuming, energy draining and life limiting.** 99
>
> Dr Michael Sinclair, Consultant Psychologist

This instinct to move away from any pain or adversity that we come into contact with in our lives takes many forms. Again, we shall be exploring these in more detail, but some common examples are:

- Avoidance – brushing things under the carpet.
- Numbing – drinking alcohol/comfort eating.
- Venting – destructive behaviour/blaming others/shouting and screaming.

The thing is, while these coping strategies are entirely natural responses to adversity – and might look, from the outside, as if the person is dealing with whatever they're going through – they're all just tactics to push it away. This only makes us feel more vulnerable and less able to cope in the long run. We haven't learnt anything and we haven't grown.

Similarly, people who rarely come up against adversity – those lives always seem to be on an even keel – may appear to be robust, but they're probably not. Think of it this way: your life only stays on an even keel if you don't take risks and embrace change. People don't take risks because they're too scared of the outcome; they can't deal with change, i.e. they're not as robust as they seem.

Truly strong people are those who are willing not to walk around pain (and by that we mean any kind of disturbance to their lives – change, adversity, trauma and upheaval) but through it. They are not afraid to sit with difficult feelings, to be curious about them instead of pushing them away. They may even welcome upheaval for the opportunities for growth that it brings as they understand that it's only by going through this process that they can become stronger.

This is the most important thing you need to remember about real strength: humans need adversity for growth, just like flowers need rain. Think of it in terms of trying to strengthen any muscle. The brain is 75% water and 25% soft tissue like any other muscle after all – and so you can train it as such. But you have to do the hard work to get the results; there are no shortcuts. It turns out that the old adage – no pain, no gain – works for our mental strength as well as our physical.

> ❝**Resilience is all about tolerance for discomfort.**❞
>
> Brené Brown, research professor, University of Houston and author of *Rising Strong*

4. Real strength is about thriving versus surviving

You may have heard some people being described as having a 'survivor' mentality, or being a 'survivor'. But real strength isn't just about surviving whatever trauma you're going through, it's about thriving because of it. It is possible – because of, and despite, setbacks – for you to become stronger and more confident and for your life to actually improve. Let's look at the difference between surviving and thriving. What do those words actually mean?

The *Oxford Dictionary* definition makes the distinction very clear:

> **Survive**: Continue to exist despite difficulty or danger; not be killed by; remain alive after the death of.

> **Thrive**: grow or develop well; prosper.

The key word here is 'grow'. Rather than seeing trauma as something to simply get through (and remain standing at the end of it), it should be seen as an opportunity to grow and learn. Not only this, but instead of wanting to hide in a dark corner until it's all over, you're then able to continue living your life according to your core values *while* going through that tough time. It's about managing to do what's important to you – to be the friend, daughter/son, partner you want to be – despite the difficult situation you may find yourself in.

> **"Tragedy doesn't have to kick your butt. Tragedy can lift you up, to take you to a higher existence."**
>
> Dr Gregg Steinberg, motivational speaker and author of *Fall Up!*

5. Real strength is about being courageous – allowing yourself to be vulnerable

You'd be forgiven for thinking that this is an oxymoron. What does vulnerability have in common with courage after all? Doesn't vulnerability mean weakness? The very opposite of courage?

But that all depends on your definition of courage …

In her TED talk, 'The Power of Vulnerability', researcher Brené Brown explains how 'courage' actually comes from *coeur*, the French word for 'heart', and that it's: 'to tell the story of who you are with your whole heart'.

We will explore vulnerability and its correlation to strength in more detail later on. For now, the crucial thing to understand is that in order to connect with your inner reserves of strength, you have to be willing to be, and to feel, vulnerable. This means being willing to show your whole self: warts, weaknesses, failings and all. It is only by doing this – allowing ourselves to be seen in all our glory – that we can truly connect with other people. And, as Brené Brown says, 'connection is what it's all about, it's why we're here'. It is also, as you'll realize while you read this book, at the very heart of real strength.

Think of the chain reaction like this:

Courage = Vulnerability = Connection = Real Strength.

If you miss out any of the links, the whole structure breaks down.

6. Real strength is about self-awareness and emotional honesty

If we look at building real strength as a journey, then being self-aware has to be the first step. It's back to those coping strategies we talked about again: most of us, if not all of us at some point in our lives, use unhelpful coping strategies to manage pain. But this then only exacerbates the problem and leaves us feeling more fragile.

If we can build self-awareness, we can better understand why we feel the way we do and behave like we do in certain situations. This understanding then gives us the opportunity and freedom to change those things about ourselves that aren't working; to stop ourselves when we begin to go down the wrong track and put ourselves on one that's going to make us feel better, sooner.

In her book *Rise: Surviving and Thriving after Trauma*, which Sian Williams wrote after a particularly traumatic time in her life (her mother was terminally ill and she was diagnosed with breast cancer), Williams writes about how resilience 'is not about ruminating and getting stuck in repetitive, negative, thoughts about why it's happened. It's more an honest exercise in self-reflection and exploration.'

Real strength is about having the self-awareness to recognize your feelings, then the courage to tell the truth about how you really feel to yourself and others. It's only when we can be truly emotionally honest like this that the real work on ourselves can start and we can begin to build strength.

It takes practice, but anyone can become more self-aware. And with self-awareness comes self-improvement and, consequently, self-respect = real strength!

7. Real strength is about emotional regulation

Emotional regulation. Management. Self-control. Whatever you want to call it, they all amount to the same thing: the ability to not let your emotions overwhelm and govern you. This is especially the case when you're going through a tough time, since more often than not this leads to behaviour which makes everything worse.

Think of it as another chain reaction:

traumatic event + a certain emotion

= a certain behaviour

= a certain picture of how we feel about ourselves

For example, imagine you get made redundant. You may feel worthless and vulnerable, so you drink to block out the pain. This then makes you unproductive the next day, so you end up doing nothing to try and find a new job. You then feel disappointed with yourself, and so the cycle of escaping pain (through drinking or whatever) and putting off actually dealing with the situation continues.

To take another example, imagine you have a huge row with your partner and he/she wants some time apart to reassess the relationship. You feel hurt and anxious that you're going to lose them, so late that night you end up calling your partner. But they aren't ready to talk and seem unreceptive. And so you end up feeling more anxious and vulnerable than you would have done had you waited until the storm had passed. Not only that but in not giving he or she the space they've asked for, you've potentially damaged the relationship further.

As we've said, nobody can stop or control traumatic events. However, if you can gain some control over the emotions that a particular event elicits, then you can begin to control – to some extent – the behaviour which follows, feeling stronger as a result.

Of course, all this takes self-awareness. If you're not aware of your emotions and when you feel them, then how can you control and manage them? With this in mind, it's useful to think of self-awareness as emotional management's big sister (she comes first!).

We'll be looking in more detail about how you can develop self–awareness and learn to regulate your emotions. In the end, however, it's only by mastering these things that you are able to live a life according to your values. Real strength and emotional regulation is about being able to rely on yourself to be the person you're meant to be.

> 66 It's not about *not* feeling those feelings, but being willing to feel them in the service of continuing to live the life you want to be living according to your values. 99

Dr Michael Sinclair, Consultant Psychologist

8. Real strength is about being optimistic

By this, we don't mean blind optimism – saying everything is going to be brilliant when it so obviously isn't! We mean realistic optimism; so hoping for the best but being prepared for the worst; aware of challenges ahead but optimistic about tackling them.

There's no denying that after a bad spell, it won't be long before there's another. Rest assured though that there will be a way through, just as a there was a way through the last challenge. Real strength is the knowledge that 'you'll handle it'. You may not know how on earth you will overcome a certain challenge or reach a goal, but you know that there is a way and you will find it – you're committed to the long haul.

> 66 Being an optimist doesn't mean being naïve, it means having belief that bad times are transient and that you have the skills to get through them. 99

Liggy Webb, consultant in behavioural skills and author of *Resilience*

However, real strength is also the ability not just to react in a healthy way to trauma (to see the positive in the situation), but also to react healthily to opportunity. If you're not able to do the latter – to first of all identify opportunities and then use them to your utmost advantage – then you're at no higher level (in terms of resilience) than if you can't react healthily to trauma.

What else does 'optimistic' mean in terms of real strength? Well, in a study carried out by psychologist Barbara Fredrickson, it was found that strong people who bounce back from negative situations are good at transforming negative feelings into positive ones. They can do this because they are emotionally complex. They don't see the world as 'black and white'; they understand that it is grey, and that very high levels of positive emotions can sit alongside negative ones.

In the study, participants were asked to write short essays about the most important problem they were facing in their lives. While resilient people reported the same amount of anxiety as less resilient people in the essays, they also revealed more happiness, interest and eagerness regarding the problem. The fact that they reported the same amount of anxiety is interesting. It means that they don't have a Pollyanna approach to life; it's not that they see everything as hunky dory, they just have a different attitude to the problem: they are optimistic about their ability to overcome it.

9. Real strength is finding sense and meaning in adversity

As well as being able to draw positive emotions from negative ones and see problems as opportunities (which we'll explore in Part 3), strong people also find meaning in adversity. In fact, it has been shown that the ability to do this makes us more resilient psychologically, and improves our physical health too.

In the late 1980s, James Pennebaker, a psychological researcher at the University of Texas in Austin, conducted an experiment with 50 healthy undergraduates. The students were asked either to write about the darkest, most traumatic, experience of their lives, or about superficial topics, for four days in a row for a period of 15 minutes each day.

Six weeks after the writing sessions, students in the trauma group reported more positive moods and fewer illnesses than those writing about everyday experiences. They also reported improved immunity and fewer visits to the student health centre. Pennebaker concluded from this experiment that confronting traumatic experiences was physically beneficial. This is because the students were processing their pain. Analysing their writing, Pennebaker noticed that they were trying to derive meaning from the trauma. They probed into the causes and consequences of the adversity and, as a result, eventually grew wiser about it. Interestingly, people who used the exercise to vent received no health benefits. There was something unique about the exercise of actual storytelling that helped people to find meaning and a silver lining.

Finding meaning can also come in the form of turning tragedy into something positive, or doing something for the greater good. For example: the parents of Isabella Peatfield who died in the Sri Lanka tsunami, who then set up a charity for Sri Lankan orphans; the man who ran the London Marathon for Cancer Research in memory of his father; the person who volunteered for Oxfam when made redundant and suddenly had time on their hands ...

All these people found sense and meaning in their trauma by doing something positive as a result of it; specifically, something that benefitted others.

"Real strength is about having the resources within ourselves to be able to bounce back from setbacks and experiences of trauma."

Dr Michael Sinclair, Consultant Psychologist

ASK YOURSELF

Q What wisdom have you gained from your traumatic experience? For example, have you come into contact with certain charities as a result of what you've been through (such as Macmillan nurses), or learnt something/gained knowledge in an area that you could pass on (such as how to navigate IVF or recover after an injury)?

Q How can you pass on that wisdom or lesson in a way that benefits others thus giving you purpose and enabling you to derive meaning from what you have been through? For example, could you start a blog about what you have experienced, or raise funds for a charity?

10. Real strength is about psychological flexibility

When we talk about psychological flexibility, we also talk about adaptability (a key component, as we've already seen, of

Resilience Engineering) and emotional agility. Psychological flexibility has many components but, at its core, it is really open-mindedness: the ability to step back from, or rise above, challenges and consider your options rather than reacting in a knee-jerk way to them. It's vital that you are not too rigid in your thinking (i.e. that you are psychologically flexible) if you want to be, and to feel, stronger, so that you can approach problem solving in a creative way.

> 66 **The most resilient people are those who are able to not just roll with the rough and the smooth, but also bend with it. If your thinking is too rigid then you won't be able to bend.** 99
>
> Liggy Webb, consultant in behavioural skills and author of *Resilience*

From a survivalist point of view, physical agility – basically the ability to move quickly, gracefully and effectively out of harm's way – is vital.

However, the same can be said of emotional agility (more of this later) in terms of surviving emotional pain.

Psychological flexibility, then, is the cousin of agility and adaptability, but is more rooted in mindfulness: the ability to sit with things in order to really see them for what they are, and then the know-how to change them and take effective action, if necessary and possible.

This is how Dr Michael Sinclair defines psychological flexibility:

"The ability to contact your present moment experience, without defence, as fully as possible as a conscious human being. To change or persist in behaviour so you can move towards the stuff you really care about in life; what you value. To be mindfully aware of thoughts and feelings and to commit to value-based living."

DR MICHAEL SINCLAIR ON 'PSYCHOLOGICAL FLEXIBILITY'

'Challenging situations will invariably trigger our stress/ fight or flight response. Our minds will produce a plethora of interpretations about the event, in the form of judging, evaluating, criticizing ourselves and others, perhaps regretting what has happened and/or worrying about the things that will happen as a consequence. As we get caught up in these products of the mind, attempting to 'problem solve' our way out of the situation and avoid any painful experiences, our ability to fully attend to the present moment is diminished. Consequently, we fail to take in new information about the circumstances around us and can also lose sight of what is really important to us, and what we might otherwise care about. Our range of coping responses becomes restricted and we fail to adapt in a fluid manner to the demands of the stressful situation. In other words, we become stuck in our ways and psychologically rigid.

Developing skills in "psychological flexibility", on the other hand, keeps us resilient; we are better able to adapt to stressful situations and their fluctuating demands on a moment-by-moment basis. We retain clarity of mind, can shift our perspective, respond to our thoughts and emotions more skillfully, recognize what matters most and behave in effective ways to manage and recover from setbacks, successfully, and in a way that feels meaningful to us.

In the context of difficult situations and setbacks, psychological flexibility is about:

- *Contacting your present moment experience as fully as possible without defence.*

- *Becoming unstuck from, and responding more effectively to stressful thoughts and feelings.*

- *Depending on the circumstances of the situation, this means choosing to change or persist in behaviour that moves you towards what you really care about in that situation; what you value, in the interests of living a fuller and more rewarding life.*

Psychological flexibility can be practised by anyone. We can all cultivate the ability to experience difficult thoughts and feelings in the service of what matters most to us. Specifically, it involves these six key skills, which are concerned with: an increased awareness ("Wake Up"); a willingness to experience difficult thoughts and feelings ("Loosen Up"); and a commitment to doing what matters most ("Step Up"):

Wake Up (Awareness)

- *Being present in the here and now, noticing thoughts and feelings as they arise (mindfulness).*

- *Being aware that you are an observer of your thoughts and feelings, that you are greater and more than your thoughts and feelings.*

Loosen Up (Willingness)

- *Unhooking yourself from stress-inducing and life-limiting thoughts; looking at your thoughts as thoughts, rather than looking at your situation through your thoughts.*

- *Accepting difficult feelings; rather than struggling to avoid, suppress or control painful feelings allowing them to come and go, as they naturally will.*

Step Up (Commitment)

- *Identifying what you really care about and what you want to stand for in this difficult situation.*

- *Taking specific and bold action, often stepping out of your comfort zone to move you closer towards what matters most.'*

11. Real strength is about balance and perspective

It can be easy to blow things out of proportion on occasion or fall into a victim mentality, thinking you're the only one that bad stuff ever happens to. Real strength, however, is about catching yourself when you do this and righting yourself again. It's about finding that balance between gauging how bad a situation really is versus how bad your anxious, panicked brain is telling you it is, after which you can respond appropriately.

ASK YOURSELF

Q Do you feel badly done to and like you have it worse than other people right now?

Q Write down three ways in which whatever challenge you are facing could be worse.

Q Can you find one positive thing to come out of whatever you are facing? Try to! Write it down.

WHAT DOES REAL STRENGTH MEAN TO YOU?

Personal strength is an ever-changing dynamic – it ebbs and flows, and we can go from feeling invincible to just coping, sometimes in the same day. It's natural to feel stronger in certain situations, when we're on 'home turf', for instance, or when we connect with a sense of certainty or purpose. But if those feelings are elusive, or the exceptions to the rule, it can be frustrating, because once you've experienced the difference that *real* strength can make to your daily life and wellbeing, why wouldn't you want to feel it more often? The first step to establishing a solid foundation of real strength is to connect with what it means to you. Take our test to find out what you are really craving when you feel like you want to be stronger.

Test by Sally Brown

QUESTION 1

Your default way of dealing with conflict is to:

A. Say what the other person wants to hear.
B. Pretend it's not happening.
C. Think about leaving.
D. Get so upset you feel ill.

QUESTION 2

You most admire people who:

A. Seem utterly fearless.
B. See the bigger picture.
C. Always speak their mind.
D. Don't panic under pressure.

QUESTION 3

At your best, you feel:

A. Like you can cope with anything.
B. Excited by the future.
C. That anything is possible.
D. That you make a difference.

QUESTION 4

In recent years, life has been:

A. A rollercoaster of change.
B. About finding myself.
C. One setback after another.
D. Terrifying at times.

QUESTION 5

When you're put on the spot at work, you:

A. Agree to anything.
B. Want to run away.
C. Find it hard to think.
D. Fight back tears.

QUESTION 6

If you felt stronger, you would:

A. Say 'yes' more often.
B. Bounce back quicker.
C. Stick to your guns.
D. Cope better with change.

QUESTION 7

As a child, you were:

A. Over-protected.
B. Determined to be top of the class.
C. A bit of a worrier.
D. Anxious to be liked.

QUESTION 8

You feel strongest when you:

A. Find a solution to a problem.
B. Stand up for what you believe in.
C. Stay calm in a time of stress.
D. Step out of your comfort zone.

QUESTION 9

Your fantasy obituary highlights your:

A. Integrity.
B. Fearlessness.
C. Resourcefulness.
D. Perseverance.

QUESTION 10

You hope that feeling stronger would make life feel less:

A. Challenging.
B. Upsetting.
C. Draining.
D. Unpredictable.

Now, add up your scores from each answer, and find out what real strength means to you, using the following table:

	A	B	C	D
Q1	4	8	6	2
Q2	8	2	4	6
Q3	2	6	8	4
Q4	6	4	2	8
Q5	4	8	6	2
Q6	8	2	4	6
Q7	2	6	8	4
Q8	6	4	2	8
Q9	4	8	6	2
Q10	8	2	4	6

If you scored between 20 and 35 …

Real strength means being resilient

For you, real strength lies in adopting a 'growth mindset', allowing you to bounce back from failure and think 'what can I learn from this?' when things go wrong. Being resilient is about having the strength to deal with stress and setbacks. By nurturing your resilience, you are more likely to hang on to your optimism in the face of setbacks.

If you scored between 36 and 45 …

Real strength means being honest

For you, strength comes from staying true to your values, to that internal compass that guides you through life's storms. Honesty and authenticity gives you the quiet strength you need to listen to your gut instinct. Right now, you are looking for strength to make difficult decisions and to do the right thing, rather than taking the path of least resistance.

If you scored between 46 and 60 …

Real strength means being adaptable

Real strength is all about your relationship with change, and how well you cope with situations that come out of the blue or that don't go the way you predicted. When you have real strength, you can embrace change with a 'bring it on!' mentality rather than avoiding it, and potentially missing out on opportunities.

If you scored between 61 and 80 …

Real strength means being brave

Real strength to you means living a big life, and having the courage to step outside your comfort zone. It's about being brave enough to be vulnerable, and being open to exploring new situations or challenges, where the risk of messing up is as great as the risk of succeeding.

CHAPTER 2

HOW ARE YOU FEELING RIGHT NOW?

I f you have recently been through, or are currently going through, a tough time then the answer is probably: 'I've been better.' Chances are you're feeling anything from anxious, vulnerable and scared, to out of your depth and depressed; you might be feeling angry about your situation, or simply like you can't cope.

When tragedy or big changes in our lives happen – anything from being diagnosed with a life-threatening illness to getting divorced – it can be very disorienting, making us question our core beliefs and experience feelings we've never felt before. There is no right or wrong way to feel, but the following are some of the most common feelings we might experience:

- No sense of normality.
- Anger and fear.
- Feeling like everything is surreal and alien.
- Feeling shut off – like you're in a box looking out on the 'normal' world.
- Feelings of 'I will never be the same again'.
- Guilt and shame heightening this sense of desperation, as you feel like you've lost control over everything.
- Loss of control itself – this can lead to acute stress.
- You can't imagine what 'strong' even feels like.
- Numb.
- Bitter and resentful.

It may be comforting to know that these feelings are not only completely normal, but they're what we're hard-wired to feel. We are not born with an aptitude for good coping strategies and psychological strength in the face of adversity. Rather, we are born with a 'survival instinct' – you may have also heard it referred to as 'the fight or flight' response. This is basically the instinct to flee, freeze or fight when we sense a threat.

"We're all born with an innate sense of vulnerablility and will all naturally try to flee from pain and adversity. It's an inherent survival tactic."

Dr Michael Sinclair, Consultant Psychologist

The survival instinct is something our primitive ancestors had to develop in order to, well, survive the daily threat to their lives. These threats were pretty big back then: attacks from sabre-toothed cats and bears or being harpooned when out shopping (i.e. hunting for food!). The trouble is, there are no longer sabre-toothed cats to fear, and we do not, generally, expect to be on high alert for fear of death when out shopping. So, the world around us has changed, but our brains have not; they have evolved to respond to *any* threat or adversity as if it *were* life threatening. This doesn't just mean modern-day physical concerns either   choosing not to take the lift in case you get stuck, or the tube in case there's a terrorist attack – but also threats to our emotional wellbeing. So that might be falling in love, attending an interview, or walking into a room full of strangers. You know the pounding heart and sweaty palm feeling you might get at such times? That's your limbic survival mode kicking in.

Our brain's natural response is to get rid of these threats in the fastest, simplest way possible (more on the ways in which we do this in a second), because the only thing on our minds is survival. But surviving despite trauma is not the same thing as *thriving* despite trauma. (As we saw in the definitions of both in Chapter 1.) The ability for the former, we are born with; the latter we have to learn, which is where this book comes in.

THE SURVIVAL INSTINCT: WHAT IS ACTUALLY HAPPENING IN OUR BRAIN WHEN WE ARE UNDER THREAT?

Before we can learn how to re-train our brains to thrive and grow through whatever life throws at us, it's helpful to know what our brains currently do when we experience adversity.

The survival instinct, or the fight or flight response, takes place in a part of the brain called the limbic system; a complex mass of nerves and networks in the middle of our heads, just behind our forehead.

The limbic system controls basic, primal emotions such as pleasure, anger, fear and hunger. Unlike the pre-frontal cortex where sophisticated reasoning and logical thinking takes place (the part of the brain we will use when developing resilience or real strength), the limbic system is far less sophisticated, and is home to primitive reactions designed simply to keep us alive. Think of it as your inner car alarm system: when it senses threat – be that physical or emotional – it goes off. 'I don't like this feeling, this pain' we say to ourselves. 'I need to get rid of it as soon as possible.'

What happens then – our body's version of the siren wailing if you like – is that our central nervous system is flooded with two main hormones: cortisol (known as the 'stress' hormone) and adrenaline – which gives us the huge surge of energy we need to either run (from those sabre-toothed cats) or to fight. It's these hormones that produce the symptoms of stress: the pounding heart and sweaty palms which ultimately force us into action.

As we touched upon in Chapter 1, these 'flight or fight' reactions or behaviours come in many forms: avoidance, rumination (more of this in a second) and venting (using a pillow as a punch bag;

shouting at your nearest and dearest!). The important thing to remember, however, is that none of these are particularly helpful – not if we want to build real strength.

Not only that, but cortisol and adrenaline are actually neuro-toxic; that is, too much of them and they can harm or even kill off brain neurons (it's true – stress shrinks our brains!) So it's in our physical and emotional health's interest to replace these stress-inducing survivalist coping strategies with more sophisticated, progressive ones that will help us to thrive.

HOW DO WE BEHAVE WHEN UNDER THREAT?

We've covered what's going on in the brain when we feel under threat, but now let's explore what behaviour this leads to. What do we actually do when trauma strikes? What are common reactions? See how many of these you recognize.

Avoidance

How many times, when faced with a difficult situation, have you tried simply to ignore it? To brush it under the carpet hoping it will just go away? (To find that it rarely does.) Sometimes, if we're going through personal tragedy, we use avoidance as a way of not having to deal with very difficult feelings. This might mean we 'dissociate' (take the attitude, *this isn't really happening to me*), point-blank ignore it and just carry on as we were before (sometimes not even telling people anything has happened); or throw ourselves into work/other areas of our lives which means we don't have to direct our focus on our pain. The problem is that often that pain will come to bite you on the bum later on, and in fact one of the biggest contributors to depression and other mental illnesses is unprocessed, un-dealt with psychological pain. If we bury it, it does us harm.

Rumination

Rumination is basically having thoughts stuck on replay and, very often, blaming ourselves for our problems. When we feel out of control in our own lives, we try to gain control by going over and over whatever's happened in our minds, trying to make some sense of it. If you've ever lain awake, asking yourself why you did such and such/why did you not do such and such, thinking I wish I'd said this, if only I'd done this, then you'll be familiar with rumination – otherwise referred to as 'dwelling' (on matters). The trouble is that the more energy we invest going over things in our heads, the less we have to find a solution or a way through.

For years, psychologists believed that we needed to vent our anger to feel happy, but actually this isn't the case. There is also scientific evidence that dwelling on things makes us feel worse.

Researchers asked people who were mildly to moderately depressed to dwell on their depression for eight minutes. The researchers found that such ruminating caused the depressed people to become significantly more depressed and for a longer period of time than people who simply distracted themselves thinking about something else. Senseless suffering – suffering that lacks hope or a silver lining – in the end leads to more depression.

In other research, BBC Lab UK together with psychologists at the University of Liverpool devised an online stress test: 32,827 people from 172 countries filled in the test which found that ruminating, brooding on our problems and self-blame, is the biggest predictor of depression and anxiety and determines the level of stress people experience. The research even suggests a person's psychological response is a more important factor than what actually happened to them. 'We found that people who didn't ruminate or blame themselves for their difficulties had much lower levels of depression and anxiety, even if they'd experienced many negative events in their lives' says Peter Kilderman, who led the study.

Self-sabotage

Self-sabotaging behaviour is behaviour that inflicts harm on us so that we don't/can't progress into what may feel like the terrifying unknown. The most common self-sabotaging behaviours include procrastination, abuse of alcohol or other substances, psychologically beating yourself up or telling yourself you're worthless (not worth looking after) as a way or an excuse to not move forward with your life.

Guilt

Guilt is really just us turning the threat on ourselves. We become the threat, not just to ourselves but to whom we imagine we have inflicted pain on. It's really just a way to not take responsibility though, or not sit with the reality of the situation (for example, if you have rejected someone, or had an affair).

Blame

Sometimes, when we're going through a really hard time, we find it too difficult to withstand and so we try to transfer it to other people. If we can blame others for what we are enduring, then we can pass up the responsibility of doing any hard work on ourselves. However, then we're stuck in a rut of blame and resentment and cannot grow from the situation.

Telling ourselves false narratives

BRENÉ BROWN ON TELLING OURSELVES FALSE NARRATIVES[1]

'Stories make us feel safe. When we are in discomfort or anxious, our brain immediately makes up a story to help us make sense of what's happening, so we can identify who the

[1] Sourced from a phone interview with Brené Brown by Katy Regan in 2015.

bad guy is (the threat) who the good guy is and how to stay safe. The brain then rewards us (with the feel good hormone dopamine) and we might feel calmer for a short while, but the problem is that the story doesn't have to be true for us to get the reward. This means that we have licence to tell ourselves any story which suits us, or more likely, gets us off the hook from feeling any pain: "This has happened at work because I/she/he is useless and disorganized etc." "It wasn't my fault that …"/"I'm not going on this date, all dates I've ever been on have been awful!"

The problem is these stories often stem from fear: fear of uncertainty, fear of what other people think of us, and are only damaging in the long run. When we're telling ourselves these stories, we're "acting out" our pain, rather than processing it. Acting out (venting) happens in the limbic brain – the less sophisticated part of the brain that is responsible for knee-jerk reactions, so we're never going to have control of that. The only thing we can do is to get back on line faster. You have to re-programme your neural pathways, strengthen them.'

As normal as they are, all these coping strategies above, unfortunately, just exacerbate pain and our feelings of fear and anxiety – making us feel weaker, not stronger. What happens then is that our pain becomes all consuming. We become obsessed with our thoughts and rumination – *why didn't I do this, if only I'd done this* – and our world shrinks because we don't have the mental space or energy to do what matters in our lives, to hold up our values. We're too busy obsessing over our pain.

THE IMPORTANCE OF BUILDING REAL STRENGTH RIGHT *NOW*

The longer you put off building your resilience, the harder it will be. Your brain is made up of hundreds of neural pathways, and the behaviours and/or thought processes we employ the most determine which of those neural pathways become strongest. (The paths with the most footfall, if you like.)

Resilience itself (building real strength) is a process, not a destination.

> **" Resilience is ... often mistakenly assumed to be a trait of the individual, an idea more typically referred to as 'resiliency.' "**
>
> Wikipedia

With this in mind, perhaps a big part of building real strength is to undo any unhelpful processes that have been reducing your resilience. This means learning to tread and strengthen new pathways, while allowing the wrong ones to grow weak. This will probably feel like hard work and there are many reasons for that:

- As we've established, we are hard-wired to employ strength-quashing coping strategies that have one goal: to survive.
- Through learned behaviour we strengthen the wrong neural pathways (translation: we get into bad habits).

- As we grow older, we become more scared of more things and therefore less resilient. Confronting our fears so we can grow becomes even more daunting.

However, let's not forget the vital point that our brains are neuroplastic, which means they are able to change and grow depending on how we choose to use them. No matter how old you are or how long you've employed unhelpful thinking patterns that don't foster resiliency, it's never too late to learn new ones. Before we find out more about how we can do this, let's look at the last point from the list above. Why is it that, if we allow it to happen, we grow less resilient as we grow older?

How come that rollercoaster-mad 7-year old has turned into a 47-year old who gets palpitations at the mere sight of a rollercoaster?

Well, not only does our limbic system act as our inner car alarm system alerting us to any threats to our wellbeing, it is also like a database of those threats. Every time we experience one – be it boarding an aeroplane or spending time alone – if our brains say 'nope, don't like that', our limbic system stores that information and it stays in the 'database' for the rest of our lives. As we continue to experience life, we add new experiences, and new information, to the limbic database of threatening situations.

The problem is, the limbic system information storage begins to have a large number of situations that cause the 'fight or flight' response. If we don't challenge this, we become scared of everything and this is how anxiety disorders can start. Before you know it, you're getting palpitations about taking tests, meeting new people, public speaking, taking lifts, or spending time alone because the limbic part of your brain has encoded this experience as something threatening. However, there's no reason why this has to happen! You can become more resilient as you age, not less – it's just knowing how.

THE POWER OF ADVERSITY: WHY GOING THROUGH SH*T IS GOOD FOR YOU!

The good news, part one

So, you've heard the bad news: we're not wired to use the best coping strategies for dealing with trauma – we have to learn them in order to become stronger. But here's the good news: this difficult patch you're going through right now – whether that be the breakdown of a relationship, divorce, bereavement, or just a general crappy time in your life – is good for you in the long run. Trauma is good for us! In fact, we can't become stronger without experiencing it, because it is the very experience of it that changes our brains.

Research has shown that right after trauma, the brain is actually more neuroplastic than usual. Neuroplasticity is the brain's ability to reorganize itself after a change in circumstances; to adjust and form new neural pathways. In short, then, we could say that right after trauma, the brain is hard-wired to perform a lot of effective healing activity. The trick is to collaborate with your brain so that you can capitalize on this – and reach your potential of what psychologists call 'post-traumatic growth'.

Post-traumatic growth and how you can encourage it

There are techniques that therapists use to encourage post-traumatic growth. This doesn't mean simply getting over whatever has happened. Rather, in the words of therapist and author of *New Ways of Seeing* Mark Tyrell, encouraging post-traumatic growth means helping people to 'look back positively at their past'; to become 'anti-fragile'. Anti-fragile is a term coined by the writer Nassim Taleb, and it means someone who is not just resilient to the stress of weight being put on them, but is strengthened by it – like bones are.

1. **Try to derive some benefit from your experience**

   Ask yourself what good things you can derive or take from your experience. Finding benefit in our trauma gives us meaning, and the meaning we attribute determines how empowered or disempowered we feel about the trauma. The worst-case scenario, for example, would be believing you are 'damaged goods' because of it.

   Instead, ask yourself: what have I learned? Not just from the trauma, but from overcoming it. So, for example, if you have been in pain over a trauma for the past ten years and are now (perhaps through therapy) feeling less so, you will have learned that everything can improve even when it feels like it never can.

2. **Recognize the powerful turning points**

   When we go through a really tough time, there is often a point at which we say to ourselves 'something has to change'. This is our 'crux' or turning point and if we can learn to listen to it, it can give us real strength and motivation to go forward. 'All fear is about loss' writes Mark Tyrrell, in his blog about therapy 'Uncommon Knowledge' (www.unk.com/blog/), 'so when you feel you have already lost everything and there is nothing else to lose, strangely fear can subside and real gains can be made.'

3. **Use metaphor**

   When we're low we often use our imagination negatively against ourselves or other people – for example, imagining the worst happening. Remembering positive metaphors (such as *How come it is, that the stone which has been thrashed about in the sea ends up being the most beautifully polished?*) helps us to use our imagination in a healthy way to feel stronger and more positive about what we've been through.

The good news, part two

Up until this point, our line has been that 'human beings are not wired to thrive' – you have to learn it. However, nothing is black and white where psychology and the science of adversity are concerned, and for every theory there is a counter argument.

So this is it – more good news! No matter how bad you're feeling right now, just like a sapling will find any chink of light and grow towards it, so will you. This process is called 'self-actualization'. Coined in the 1950s by psychologist Carl Rogers, to self-actualize is 'to fulfill ones potential and achieve the highest level of "human beingness" we can'. In other words, be the best and the strongest we can be. Rogers believed this to be our sole motive in life. If this is true, it should be very reassuring to know that the simple fact you are human means you will, eventually, naturally find your way to the light, overcoming whatever situation you're in.

Professor Stephen Joseph of Nottingham University specializes in the study and research around human flourishing and wellbeing. Here he talks about the 'self-actualization' theory, a theory created by Abram Maslow. 'Self-actualization' means the growth of an individual towards the 'ultimate fulfillment of the highest needs'. In other words, growing towards being the very best person you can be, fulfilling (especially) the need to find meaning in life.

'We tend to react to adversity as "biological organisms"', says Professor Joseph. 'We grow because we want to regain the sense of who we are and our biological instincts are to thrive and to be resilient, to grow and reassess our place in the world, to develop and strengthen our relationships.'

So, in this chapter we have looked at the 'science of adversity'. We have explored what is going on in your brain when you come up against it, and how it's likely to be making you feel at the moment. It goes without saying that life can throw us some pretty tough times, and none of us escape at least some adversity in our lives. As we have said, however, it is how you cope with these challenges that's the important thing. There is a body of evidence, both anecdotal and scientific, that says you can grow from these experiences. Adversity can be a springboard for not just a good life, but a better, more meaningful one, and you can – you will – come out stronger.

ASK YOURSELF

Q How are you feeling right now about the challenges you are currently facing? Make a list of five core emotions you're experiencing.

Q How are these feelings making you behave? Are you ruminating (going over and over things in your mind); trying to numb feelings by pushing them away and avoiding them; or are you 'venting' – perhaps taking out your emotions on other people?

Q Consider how you felt and reacted to past traumas.

Q Identify and write down two unhelpful strategies you have employed and which you can now concentrate on trying to replace with better, more helpful ones.

HOW DO YOU DEAL WITH ADVERSITY?

There's more to real strength than simply coping with adversity. But we can't get away from the fact that adversity plays a big part in shaping who we are. An increasing body of research is showing that strength can come from trauma, if we react in the right way. But for some of us, adversity is overwhelming and undermining, and recovering from it takes time and effort. When we're faced with an acute crisis, your autonomic nervous system takes over and the fight-or-flight response kicks in. But longer term challenges require a different kind of processing. Understanding how and why challenging times undermine our sense of wellbeing and equilibrium is the first step to taking control.

Test by Sally Brown

QUESTION 1

When bad things happened during childhood, you tended to:

A. Have a tantrum and create a scene.

B. Retreat to your room and not tell anyone.

C. Plaster on a smile and get on with it.

D. Escape into a fantasy world.

QUESTION 2

When you think about challenges ahead, you:

A. Feel yourself shrinking inside.

B. Would rather not think about it.

C. Think about running away.

D. Start to feel hot and bothered.

QUESTION 3

People know you're under pressure because you:

A. Eat or drink more.

B. Start talking about holidays.

C. Are on a short fuse.

D. Are quieter than usual.

QUESTION 4

Stress has the biggest impact on your:

A. Peace of mind.

B. Relationships.

C. Social life.

D. Health.

QUESTION 5

When you're under pressure, help from other people:

A. Can make things easier, if they don't wind you up.
B. Is appreciated, but you tend to sort yourself out.
C. Is unusual, because you look like you're coping.
D. Can make you feel guilty, like you've failed.

QUESTION 6

At work, you've got a reputation for:

A. Keeping your head down and getting on with things.
B. Being relentlessly upbeat.
C. Always planning your next holiday.
D. Being prepared to fight your corner.

QUESTION 7

You can cope with most things, as long as you;

A. Can convince yourself everything's OK.
B. Have something to look forward to.
C. Got the help you need.
D. Have time alone to think things through.

QUESTION 8

You would feel upset by people thinking:

A. You're flaky.
B. You can't cope.
C. You're boring.
D. You're a bully.

QUESTION 9

You are involved in a minor car accident that isn't your fault. Your first instinct would be to:

A. Give the other person a hard time.
B. Get home so you can calm yourself down.
C. Reassure everyone that you're completely fine.
D. Think about buying a new car.

QUESTION 10

Which of these emotions/habits most undermines your wellbeing?

A. Rumination.
B. Thinking you're invincible.
C. Catastrophizing.
D. Losing your temper.

Now, add up your scores from each answer, and find out how you deal with adversity, using the following table:

	A	B	C	D
Q1	2	4	6	8
Q2	4	6	8	2
Q3	6	8	2	4
Q4	8	2	4	6
Q5	2	4	6	8
Q6	4	6	8	2
Q7	6	8	2	4
Q8	8	6	4	2
Q9	2	4	6	8
Q10	4	6	8	2

If you scored between 20 and 35 ...

You deal with adversity by lashing out

Anger is your defence against adversity – when you feel attacked, either by other people or simply the environment around you, you fight back. You may be prone to anxiety, or live in a state of permanently raised stress and hypervigilance. It may have caused you relationship problems in the past because you tend to blame others for your problems, and can say hurtful things in anger to people you love.

If you scored between 36 and 45 ...

You deal with adversity by hiding away

Your instinct is to shy away from conflict, and deal with challenges and difficulties by retreating into yourself until you can make sense of them in your head. Loved ones know when you're under pressure because you go quiet. You're generally self-contained and are good at managing your emotions, but sometimes internalizing your problems impacts on your mood and resilience, especially if you have a tendency to ruminate.

If you scored between 46 and 60 ...

You deal with adversity by pretending everything is OK

You may have been brought up to 'not make a fuss' and believe pretending everything is 'just fine' is a commendable character trait. But denial or disassociating from your feelings never leads to real strength. Instead, it creates a flimsy façade that can crumble, so you need to use over drinking or eating to help numb your feelings. Your first step to building real strength is to get in touch with your feelings and emotions rather than rejecting them.

If you scored between 61 and 80 ...

You deal with adversity by running away

As an 'all-or-nothing' thinker and a catastrophizer, you can be convinced there is no other option but to walk away from your problems and start again. But by abandoning that difficult relationship or job, you never get the chance to properly process and understand your emotions. It's time to trust your ability to survive difficult times so you can learn from your experience, and prove to yourself that you can deal with adversity.

CHAPTER 3

MOVING TOWARDS REAL STRENGTH

W e've talked about how you might be feeling right now and why; what happens in our brains when we hit a tough patch and how this translates into behaviour. We also understand how, if we employ unhealthy coping strategies again and again – if we make a habit out of dwelling or venting or numbing – then these become learnt behaviours. Our brains literally tell us to go down these well-trodden paths. But we can learn different behaviours and go down different paths! Ones that increase our feelings of security and strength. In short, when it comes to building real strength, we're in charge. So how can we prepare ourselves? How do we actually lay down the foundations for real strength?

GROW A GROWTH MINDSET

When you hear the word 'mindset' you may think of it as a synonym for 'attitude', and you'd be right. But did you know that in psychological terms, just two mindsets, two attitudes to life if you like, have been identified: the 'fixed' and 'growth' mindset. Out of these two mindsets, which we manifest from a very early age, springs a great deal of our behaviour, our relationship with success and failure and ultimately our capacity for happiness and real strength.

The concept of mindset – and the fact that all of us have either a 'fixed' one or a 'growth' one – is a very simple but effective idea developed by Stanford University psychologist Carol Dweck after decades of research into success and achievement. Dweck wanted to find out why – if you took a group of people who had the same talents, skills and resources – some of them achieved, often excelling in their field, and others fell by the wayside, even dropping out entirely.

Let's look at both mindsets in more detail. What do they mean? How might they affect the way you live your life and, ultimately, your ability to thrive despite setbacks?

A fixed mindset

Put very simply, those with a fixed mindset think that their basic qualities – such as intelligence, talents and skills – are 'fixed'. They believe that what they were given at birth is all there will ever be, and so tend to spend their time documenting these skills and level of intelligence, rather than developing them, believing this to be futile.

The fixed mindset is all about judging – *This means I am/I don't/I can't*. They also believe that success is merely the 'affirmation' of inherent strengths they already possess, rather than evidence of how much they have, and can grow. They believe that innate talent alone creates success – not effort. But they're wrong!

A growth mindset

People with a growth mindset understand that having brains and talent is a good starting point, but also that nobody ever accomplishes things without passion and hard work.

They believe simply that they can grow their brain's capacity to learn and improve and that failure is all part of this process. The very fact that they are not just willing to fail, but see failure as an essential platform for thriving, means that people with a growth mindset are naturally more resilient and strong. And so it follows, if you want to develop inner strength, it's very important to work on developing this.

CAN I DEVELOP OR LEARN A GROWTH MINDSET?

The answer is definitely 'yes'. In fact, a growth mindset is already being taught in worlds of business, education and sport, developing motivation and productivity, enhancing resilience and relationships. This is because, just like thriving, it's all about growth and learning, rather than winning. Someone with a fixed mindset thinks: *what's the point in anything unless I am the best?* The person with a growth mindset, on the other hand, thinks: *how can I improve? Be better? Learn from this situation?*

HOW TO GROW FROM A FIXED TO A GROWTH MINDSET

In *Grit: Passion, Perseverance and the Science of Success,* American psychologist Angela Duckworth discusses what differentiates people who achieve outstandingly in their field from those who don't. What she found was that it has nothing to do with IQ or talent, but a special blend of perseverance and passion: grit. Furthermore, those with grit all had a 'growth mindset' and couldn't be gritty without it.

In an article on grit vs. resilience which also touches on Duckworth's research, happiness expert Tamara Lechner suggests the following five tips:[1]

1. Choose your language carefully

The language you use when praising someone can make the difference between developing a growth or a fixed mindset. When you praise someone for a characteristic or strength (for example: 'you are really smart', 'you are so flexible'), it teaches a fixed mindset. Whereas if you praise for effort or strategy – 'you worked so hard at that painting' – it teaches a growth mindset and reinforces the individual's role in the successful outcome.

2. Surround yourself with positive people

It's pretty obvious, but the attitude of those around you can really affect your own mood and attitude. By

[1] www.chopra.com/articles/resilience-and-grit-how-to-develop-a-growth-mindset.

surrounding yourself with 'can do' people who believe that with passion and persistence they can achieve things, this growth mindset becomes the norm and rubs off onto you.

3. Be flexible with your thinking

Becoming less rigid in your thoughts and actions allows resilience and grit to blossom simply because flexible people don't see problems; they see opportunities for growth and learning. When every challenge is met with creative thinking, you feel more capable and confident, and this all breeds resilience.

4. Set goals that align with your purpose

People with purpose – i.e. a reason for doing things – are happier. If you create goals which reflect what really matters to you (making more time for family, spending more time doing creative pursuits), success comes more easily and quicker.

5. Build time into your day for reflection

When you take time to reflect, you bring awareness to the things you have accomplished and what you want to focus on next. Whether you meditate, write down your thoughts or go for a walk, when you give yourself time to assess your life in a non-judgemental way, it empowers you to make choices about what to do next.

Like most skills worth having, resilience and grit take practice and persistence. Part of having a 'growth mindset', however, is believing this is possible! That with effort, you can get better at a certain skill. As you will discover, if you put in the practice and the work, you will reap rewards in every area of your life.

THE POWER OF GRIT

We shall be talking a lot more about the power of grit, what it is and how you can develop, it in Chapter 8. For the meantime, however, it's enough to tell you that grit – or should we say, gritty people – share very similar, if not the same, traits as those with a growth mindset. A bit like how resilience and strength go hand in hand, so do grittiness and growth mindset; so it figures that if you're laying down the foundations for real strength, it's a good idea to understand and foster both.

What is 'grit' anyway?

Interestingly, the author of *Grit*, Angela Duckworth, who developed the idea, had very similar research objectives to Carol Dweck: to find out why some people – given the same talent, intelligence and resources – accomplish more than other individuals.

As part of her research, in the summer of 2004, she went to study 1200 army cadets who were just about to begin the 'Beast Barracks'– an infamous seven-week grueling training course where candidates would toil for 17 hours a day with no break. Some dropped out, but Duckworth wanted to find out why this was and why some people endured the course.

'Scientists have tried to solve this puzzle for more than 50 years,' writes Duckworth. 'But even the school's best means of screening its applicants – something called the "whole candidate score," a weighted mixture of a student's SATs, high school ranking, leadership ability, and physical fitness – does not anticipate who will succeed and who will fail at Beast.'

And so, Duckworth designed her own way of scoring candidates, giving each a survey that tested his or her willingness to persevere in pursuit of long-term goals. She called this measure 'grit'. And it worked! The cadets' answers helped predict whether they would make it through the grueling 'Beast Barracks' to the bitter end.

66 Grit is living life like a marathon, not a sprint. 99

Angela Duckworth, author of *Grit*

Although grit and resilience share many of the same qualities, what differentiates grit, perhaps, is the requirement for 'passion'. Resilience is having the optimism and the ability to get back up after a setback, whereas grit is having the *passion* and the perseverance to carry on with a task or challenge over a long period of time.

Taking this into consideration, as you prepare yourself mentally to build real strength, it's probably a good idea to set aside some time to thinking about how you can do this with passion. What motivates you? What are you passionate about? How can you connect with this passion (or passions) to not just overcome the adversity you're going through, but to stick with it for as long as it takes?

ARE YOU READY *AND* WILLING?

66 In order to grow from painful experiences and feelings, there needs to be an increased willingness to experience these feelings without putting up defences. 99

Dr Michael Sinclair, Consultant Psychologist

So you now hopefully have a better idea about what real strength actually is and how you might prepare yourself to cultivate more of it. The very act of thriving also rests upon your willingness to go through pain. Just like working on any muscle, strengthening your psychological one is going to take effort and perseverance, not to mention mastering some skills, so it's essential you're not just ready, but absolutely WILLING.

But let's look for a moment about what 'willing' actually means. How can we describe this attitude to the changes you're about to make? And how can you be sure you have it?

First, 'being willing' to sit with discomfort and difficult feelings is not the same thing as 'tolerating' them.

DR MICHAEL SINCLAIR ON 'WILLINGNESS'

'There's a big difference between tolerating a feeling and being "willing". Willing is the opposite of attempting to control, suppress or reduce unwanted feelings. When we are tolerating a feeling, we are often waiting for it to pass and wishing it would as soon as possible.

Willingness involves a genuine openness and curiosity to this experience: Let me notice it, let me notice how it waxes and wanes … How it rises and falls … because all feelings do change over time. The more time you calmly observe them, rather than trying to escape or reduce them, the more you are in control of your actions and can engage in your life in meaningful ways.

It's important to remind yourself: my experience tells me, when I'm willing to have the feeling and allow it to do its thing, then I have less distress in the long run and I get more done. There is an alternative to fighting it.

It's like struggling in quick sand. Everything we've learnt, which is evolutionarily wired to know about escaping, is causing us to sink deeper. We need to learn that if we stay still, albeit counterintuitive, we give ourselves opportunities to see alternative routes out. You don't have to struggle. Do nothing.'

This, by the way, is the great thing about willingness, and should be a big motivation for sitting with emotions rather than reverting to type and pushing them away: the more you're able to sit with emotions, the less distress you will have in the long run and the faster the trauma will be over.

So, simply staying still and letting the feelings wash over us is one way we can show willing when it comes to accepting adversity in our lives, but there are other things too.

- Use mindfulness to be present with your pain: 'You've got to crank up your willingness and this means practising how to be present with it, we need to use mindful breath to stay present and notice the feelings,' says Dr Sinclair.

- If it's the loss of dreams or ambitions that's causing your current pain, be willing to grieve: 'I think one of the reasons we don't let go of certain narratives – is because we have to grieve in order to move through it,' says Brené Brown, author of *Rising Strong*. She explains how we sometimes prefer to stay in a place of longing or resentment because those emotions have what she calls 'agency' – we're cross! And so what keeps us stuck in those narratives sometimes is the unwillingness to walk through what has to be walked through. But staying in anger and bitterness is more difficult than confronting our grief. Our fear of it is often far worse than the reality.

ASK YOURSELF

Q Which describes you best: a gritty person – i.e.
someone who has passion and the ability to persevere
with things for a long time; or a resilient person – i.e.
someone who bounces back from difficulties?

Q What are you passionate about? What one thing gives
you purpose and meaning in life? A challenge that you
feel you would be willing to stick with, through thick
and thin?

HOW DO YOU DEAL WITH UNCOMFORTABLE FEELINGS?

'Emotional management' is one of the keys to developing inner strength. How we deal with the difficult feelings that are part and parcel of life impacts on our moods, optimism and resilience. It's human nature to dislike uncomfortable feelings, because the brain equates negative emotions with danger. So rather than 'sitting with' our feelings of worry, guilt, shame, apprehension or fear – and learning from them – we put all our efforts into changing our emotional state. But there are different ways to process feelings, and some are more helpful than others. Here's how to identify your instinctual approach to uncomfortable feelings, and why it works for you.

Test by Sally Brown

QUESTION 1

You leave an important work meeting feeling like you messed up. Your default reaction is to:

A. Think about what you need to do differently next time.
B. Turn it into a funny story to tell your friends.
C. Put it out of your mind and focus on your next task instead.
D. Treat yourself to a break and your favourite coffee while you calm down.

QUESTION 2

Your go-to way to boost your mood is to:

A. Spend time with an upbeat person.
B. Move your body with a walk, run or a yoga class.
C. Give yourself an encouraging pep talk.
D. Meditate or take some time out to calm yourself.

QUESTION 3

You know your feelings have got on top of you when you feel:

A. Ambivalent about your usual interests.
B. Self-critical or self-doubting.
C. Out of touch with a sense of purpose.
D. Irritable and lose your sense of humour.

QUESTION 4

Experience has taught you that to feel happy, you need to:

A. Tune into your body and take care of yourself.
B. Keep growing as a person.
C. Take yourself and life lightly.
D. Nurture your imagination.

QUESTION 5

You know you'll be OK as long as you:

A. Keep learning.
B. Keep laughing.
C. Keep moving.
D. Keep calm.

QUESTION 6

You feel your most authentic when you're:

A. Helping other people feel happy.
B. So immersed in an activity you lose track of time.
C. Thinking about being your best self.
D. Growing as a person.

QUESTION 7

People would be surprised to find out how much you:

A. Need to exercise to stay sane.
B. Care about making the world a better place.
C. Doubt yourself at times.
D. Worry about life in general.

QUESTION 8

Which statement do you most agree with?

A. You can cope with anything if you're kind to yourself.
B. There is something to learn from every experience.
C. Seeing the funny side can get you through most things.
D. Distracting yourself can give you a sense of perspective.

QUESTION 9

Your gut instinct tells you:

A. When something doesn't feel right.

B. When it's time to loosen up.

C. When you need to boost your mood.

D. When you need some me-time.

QUESTION 10

Your biggest barrier to happiness is:

A. Not spending enough time with friends.

B. Not making time for exercise.

C. Feeling so tired you neglect yourself.

D. Feeling stuck with no sense of purpose.

Now, add up your scores from each answer, and find out how you deal with uncomfortable feelings, using the following table:

	A	B	C	D
Q1	2	4	6	8
Q2	4	6	8	2
Q3	6	8	2	4
Q4	8	2	4	6
Q5	2	4	6	8
Q6	4	6	8	2
Q7	6	8	2	4
Q8	8	2	4	6
Q9	2	4	6	8
Q10	4	6	8	2

If you scored between 20 and 35 ...

Curiosity helps you deal with difficult feelings

You're interested in how your mind works, so rather than ignoring difficult feelings, you treat them as a source of information. You may have an interest in mindfulness that has taught you the value of being curious about feelings and exploring them without attaching judgement to them. It's the basis of a 'growth mindset' that allows you to learn from adversity. Whether it's an instinctive mindset for you or something you've learned, it will form the basis of your resilience and inner strength.

If you scored between 36 and 45 ...

Humour helps you deal with difficult feelings

Humour is your best defence as it helps you get uncomfortable feelings in proportion and feel in control again. It's also a way to diffuse group tension and get people talking. You are adept at using humour as a kind way to get your point across when you feel someone has let you down or annoyed you. Sometimes, people can accuse you of never taking anything seriously but they're missing the point – it's because you can be so deeply affected by things that you need humour for self-protection.

If you scored between 46 and 60 ...

Distraction helps you deal with difficult feelings

Taking your mind off things is your default way to start to process uncomfortable feelings, whether that's using exercise, throwing yourself into work or a hobby, or simply meeting up with friends and talking about other things. Distraction gives you the distance you need to look at what you're feeling and where it's come from without reacting to it.

If you scored between 61 and 80 ...

Self-compassion helps you deal with difficult feelings

It may have been a hard-won battle, but you've come to a place where you understand that you have to be your own best friend. So when uncomfortable feelings hit, you're most likely to ask yourself, 'What do I need right now to get through this? How can I support myself?' You're also good at not judging or criticizing yourself for bad decisions.

2 WHAT'S STOPPING YOU FROM BOUNCING BACK?

CHAPTER 4

ARE SOME PEOPLE MORE RESILIENT THAN OTHERS?

I t's the million-dollar question isn't it? Why do some people seem more able to deal with and overcome adversity, while others crumble?

Scientists have been studying this for years. Specifically, they have looked at the difference between 'orchid' children and 'dandelion' children. This is a metaphor developed by the Scandinavians. The general consensus behind it being that a 'dandelion child' can remain healthy and survive in harsh environments, but might remain average or unremarkable (like a weed). Orchids, on the other hand, require protection and shelter to thrive. However, under the right conditions and with nurturing, when an 'orchid child' fully blossoms he or she is extraordinary.

Excitingly, in 2015, scientists from Duke University made a breakthrough discovery. They identified a specific gene variant linked to 'orchid' children who are highly sensitive to their environments and are particularly vulnerable to stress. The genetic marker is part of the glucocorticoid receptor gene NR3C1 that influences the activity of a receptor to which cortisol binds and is directly involved in the stress response.

In another study, it was identified that the children who carried the NR3C1 gene variant were much more likely to develop serious problems in adulthood if they did not receive special support services.

If left untreated, 75% of high-risk 'orchid' children with the NR3C1 gene variant went on to develop psychological problems by age 25. These behaviours included substance abuse, aggression and antisocial personality disorder.

The good news, however, is that when children with this gene variant participated in intensive support services, only 18% developed problems as adults.

It's a hopeful finding ... Far from being doomed, the children particularly sensitive to stress were also particularly responsive to help and had the capacity to become highly resilient, leading members of society, with the right nurturing, loving kindness, empathy and social connection.

Another recent study by Heather Rusch at the National Institute of Health's National Institute of Nursing Research revealed two critically important factors associated with resilience in the face of adversity, and the good news is that they are both under our control.

In the study, 159 women who had endured serious physical assault were given a questionnaire designed to gauge their current and past levels of post-traumatic stress disorder and other psychiatric conditions, as well as various measures of resilience, social support, personality and quality of life.

The positive news is that 79% did not develop post-traumatic stress disorder (PTSD) following the assault. The most negative outcome was depression, which affected 30%. The researchers then divided respondents to the questionnaire into three categories:

1. Those who had never been diagnosed with a psychiatric disorder.
2. Those who had been in the past but had recovered.
3. Those who were currently diagnosed with a psychiatric disorder.

What they found was that those who had recovered and had never been diagnosed had two qualities in common: mastery and social support.

Mastery refers to the degree to which individuals perceive themselves as having control and influence over life circumstances. This is not the same as optimism, which is the expectation of positive outcomes. Interestingly, mastery – not optimism – is the better predictor of resilience in the face of trauma.

The second factor, social support, was also crucially important. But the emphasis is on 'support'. Respondents who reported strong supportive social ties were less likely to develop psychiatric disorders and more likely to recover from them if they did. In contrast, unsupportive, unreceptive and critical responses from friends, family or coworkers actually increased the risk to PTSD survivors. The researchers believe the negative impact likely arises from attempts to discourage open communication, which increases cognitive avoidance and suppression of trauma-related memories, social withdrawal and self-blame.

" We all have the ability to cultivate resilience. "

Dr Michael Sinclair, Consultant Psychologist

Consultant Counselling Psychologist Dr Michael Sinclair relays that if you've dealt with trauma in the past using unhelpful coping mechanisms (such as avoidance), it could make you less resilient going forward. On the other hand, if you learn from these experiences instead, it could help you a great deal in the future. Imagine you suffered a trauma in your youth, such as losing a parent or being bullied. If your coping strategy then was to bottle up your emotions – but you learnt that this was unhelpful – you may well have discovered a healthier strategy which would most likely serve you well in the future. You had to experience the trauma, however, in order to make that discovery – hence why it's *how* you dealt with traumas, and what you learned, that determines how resilient you're likely to be in the future.

With this in mind, we can understand how, if you take two individuals who suffered childhood abuse, one might grow up to be an incredibly resilient adult and the other incredibly vulnerable, depending on the coping strategies they used. Equally, just because you've had a relatively easy life so far, it doesn't mean you will crumble at the first hint of trauma. You may be genetically predisposed to positive re-framing of situations and creative thinking, which will make you naturally manage the situation better when something does happen.

It is also a common misapprehension that resilient people don't have negative emotions or thoughts, remaining optimistic in most or all situations. On the contrary, resilient people have just developed proper coping techniques over time and are able to balance negative emotions with positive ones. As a result, they don't tend to over-react to difficult situations.

The key phrase in that paragraph is 'over time'. When trying to answer the question of whether some people are more resilient than others, it's crucial to remember that even though some people may have a natural or nurture-based leaning towards real strength, it's not a rare quality and anyone can develop it when they know how.

So, we've already heard a bit about how genetic factors and past experiences affect your ability to be mentally strong. However, there are a few things – a few core qualities if you like – without which, you're going to struggle. Put another way, there are some qualities that all strong people possess, that lay the perfect foundations from which strength can grow. We've identified these as:

1. Having deep values.
2. Passion.
3. Purpose.

We already touched upon all three in Part 1, but let's take each one in turn, and look at it in more depth.

1. IDENTIFY AND DEFINE YOUR VALUES

Dr Michael Sinclair defines a value as a 'freely chosen, global quality of ongoing action'. Basically, values are not goals – they are the qualities we want to bring to the actions we take as we go about our life in the many different contexts and roles we have. We can set ourselves value-based goals and take committed action towards these. They inform how we're going to do it, and why. For example, in terms of overcoming struggles, a goal might be: I want to get through this adversity, but the value might be: by being kinder to myself or by being a calmer mother while I do it. Taken at their most base level, 'values' are what matters to us. When we take the time and trouble to find that out, and then live our lives accordingly, we feel much stronger inside and more self-confident.

Susan David is a clinical psychologist and author of the book *Emotional Agility*. In her TED talk of the same name, she says, 'What makes the most difference to our lives and our happiness are the habits we create that are imbued with our values.' She goes on to talk about the importance of having values that are linked to our 'want to' goals rather than our 'have to' goals, if we want to stay strong – and how resilient people understand that. Your 'want to' goals, she explains, are basically your personal reasons for achieving those goals, whereas your 'have to' goals are more about other peoples' opinions and what you feel society expects from you. To relay an example David uses in her talk, of the struggles we come up against, imagine you are trying to lose weight. Then you open the fridge to find a huge piece of chocolate cake. Our chances of resisting the cake, she explains, have nothing to do with willpower. Willpower alone won't keep you from eating it. However, if you can tune into your *value* or *values* informed by your 'want to' goals, rather than your 'have to' goals, you stand a much higher chance of being strong and resisting temptation.

A 'have to goal' in this situation might be: 'I *have* to resist the chocolate cake and lose weight otherwise people are going to judge me at the school reunion I'm going to next month.'

Your 'want to goal' on the other hand might be: 'I *want* to be able to look and feel good about myself at the school reunion, so I'll resist the chocolate cake.'

Our relationship to temptation becomes different when informed by our values. These are informed by our 'want to goals', so it makes sense to identify them – even to write them down.

ASK YOURSELF

 In my current struggle, what is my 'want to' goal?

 Is this choice of how I am reacting to my struggle bringing me closer to the person I want to be?

 Could I choose an alternative behaviour that would bring me closer?

If you were to think of your struggles like a stormy sea, then your values are like rocks to cling to. They are the things that help you to hold on, even when you're being bashed about by high waves; the things that keep your feet fixed on the ground. Your values are what should be important to you and what matters. They can be specific to whatever struggle you are going through (for example, *I'm trying to lose weight*), or more relevant to your life and how you live it in general (for example, *I value being a good friend*). It is a good idea to define both in your life: a list of ongoing values for your life in general and more specific ones relating to what's happening in your life at present. The most important thing to remember is that the strongest people are able to uphold their values *no matter* what else is happening in their lives. So make yours as deep as possible.

LIGGY WEBB ON DEFINING YOUR VALUES

'What am I for? How often do you take time to stop and think and explore the answer to that question? Do you truly know what you value and what gives you a strong foundation and purpose in your life?

A great place to start is by having a clear understanding of your values. Values are essentially what's important to us. Each person's values are of course unique because even if two people choose the same value word, each person will have a different interpretation of what that actually means to them and how they demonstrate this.

Our values reflect who we are on a daily basis and in everything that you do.

So how do you identify your values?

Here are six steps:

1. *Find a quiet space for at least 45 minutes to stop and think without any external distractions whatsoever.*

2. *Write down the three proudest achievements of your life as if you were writing them in a letter to a friend. Describe the impact they had on you, and on other people. How did you feel? What kind of feedback did you get?*

3. *Now explore what core personal behaviours helped you to achieve the success. What was it exactly that you did?*

4. *Read through what you have written for each example and highlight any common behaviours that you demonstrated, i.e. integrity, kindness, honesty, authenticity, boldness, authenticity, fairness …*

5. *Now pick the values that you identify as the most important to you and work out what you do on a regular basis to reinforce these values.*

6. *Check in with yourself on a regular basis to establish that you are staying true to your values. Ask yourself if the decisions you make on a day-to-day basis are representative of what you truly value and hold dear.'*

2. DISCOVER YOUR PASSION

In Part 1, we talked a little about passion (in particular, how it is a vital component to grit). It's much easier to be strong if you are passionate about whatever challenge you're facing. For example, making it to the end of a tough training programme at work, or finishing writing a novel. If you're looking to develop your strength or grit, one way would be to surround yourself with passionate people; passion breeds passion after all.

Passion is also probably the one factor that differentiates grit from resilience. Grit is not just about bouncing back, it's about being able to keep going – and passion is your motivator.

Finding your passion will reveal where you want to direct your energy and guide your goals. It's the fuel for the fire in your belly, as well as the fuel for this journey you have embarked upon: from trauma to triumph.

Growing your passion

It's important to understand that when we talk about passion in terms of grit and real strength, we don't mean intense emotion or emotional fireworks. Rather, we mean something that burns long and hard – we mean consistent attention and focus on something over time.

So what *is* your passion?

Many people find it hard to answer this question. Some people find themselves pursuing lots of different goals, but are not actually sure about their 'passion'. In these instances, something called 'a goal hierarchy' can help, because it enables you to split up your goals into bite-sized chunks. This then helps you to see whether those goals serve a common purpose – that common purpose being your true passion.

The goal hierarchy

The 'goal hierarchy', or 'GBS' goal breakdown structure, was developed by Joseph M. Juran in his *Quality Control Handbook*. It was originally used for project management in a business context, but has been adapted by coaches and psychologists alike for individuals. The goal hierarchy comprises of three 'tiers' of goal: low-level, mid-level and top-level.

1. **Low-level goal:** This is specific and short term, such as getting to work 15 minutes earlier each day in order to get more done. You want to achieve this short-term goal as it lays foundations for the next level, which is your ...

2. **Mid-level goal:** This is the next milestone you need to arrive at after achieving the low-level goal. So, for example, if your low-level goal is getting to work earlier each day, your mid-level goal might be getting one more task on your to-do list done every day, for six weeks.

3. **Top-level goal:** The goals at the top of the hierarchy are abstract, general and should be your 'ultimate concern'. There can only be one of these top-level goals and it serves as a compass and gives meaning to all the lower-level goals – for example, (in this circumstance), your top-level goal might be to get promoted.

Passion is about being loyal to your 'ultimate concern' and being gritty means holding your ultimate goal for a long time, so you can better make the 'ultimate concern' something you really, really want! Passion is like the compass that guides you to where you want to be. It keeps you focused and strong during a tough challenge.

ASK YOURSELF

Ⓠ What do I care about?

Ⓠ Who do I want to help the most?

Ⓠ When do I feel most engaged with what I am doing?

Ⓠ How would I use a gift of a million pounds if it had to be given away?

3. CONNECT TO YOUR PURPOSE

We already touched upon the importance of purpose in Chapter 3 when we talked about developing a growth mindset. We looked at how having purpose was vital for that, for believing that with effort (and purpose!) things can improve. So what *is* purpose?

In very basic terms, it is a reason for doing something: as in, my purpose for going to town is to go to the bank, or my purpose for calling my mum is to ask her when is next convenient for me to visit her. In terms of 'purpose' in the context of real strength, however, it is your central, motivating aim; it's the reason you get up in the morning.

Purpose, and living with purpose, feels like you are doing something you were made for. It feels authentic and makes you feel alive. Ever been cooking or writing or looking after someone and felt entirely content, like you've lost track of time? That's living with purpose.

Purpose guides life decisions and can influence behaviour; it can shape goals, offer a sense of direction and create meaning. Therefore, having it is not just good for resilience, it's vital.

It's important to remember that purpose, too, is different for everyone. Some people find purpose in their job or vocation in life, some in their friendships and relationships, and some in spiritual or religious journeys.

Also, your purpose can shift and change at different times of your life, depending on what's happening. It tends to be readdressed at times of adversity and big changes. This, then, is one of the major upsides of struggle. Struggles force us to re-evaluate our lives and whether or not we're living them as we wish. They give us an opportunity to curate a better, happier life.

So, how can you find your purpose?

ASK YOURSELF

 When do I feel fulfilled?

 Where do I feel I belong?

 Who am I? What stokes my fire?

66 Resilience is about learning to identify and let go of bad habits and finding smarter ways of doing things. 99

Liggy Webb, consultant in behavioural skills and author of *Resilience*

Purpose – and finding it – can be about long-term goals and long-term visions, but there are also things we can do to live our day-to-day lives in a purpose-filled way. Some of the ways in which you might do this are:

- **Reflecting:** At the end of each day, think about and make a mental note about your day. Which parts made you feel alive and which parts drained you? For example, you might find that seeing certain people gave you a boost, but that spending time on social media brought your mood down. If you have a record of this, you can do something about it

- **Practising gratitude:** Before you go to bed, write down three good things that you are thankful for today. They don't need to be hugely eventful to help you find your purpose; the important thing is to notice patterns. For example, over the course of a month, you might find that the 'three good things' you are thankful for are often to do with spending time with your family, or to do with your work. These, then, are your purpose.

- **Paying attention to dreams:** It is often in your dreams that your conscious mind works on issues that you may or may not have yet consciously acknowledged. Dreams are almost never prophetic, but they can provide really valuable insights into your personal needs, desires and concerns. For example, one common dream is being chased. This is believed to mean that in your waking, day-to-day life, you are currently running away from something which is causing you anxiety and that you need to pay attention to.

One of the common features among people who live with purpose is that they are able to find meaning in things that happen to them. Andrew Zolli, author of *Resilience*, describes these people as being able to 'cognitively reappraise situations and regulate emotions, turning life's proverbial lemons into lemonade'.

However, having a strong sense of purpose is not just beneficial to our emotional and mental wellbeing, it's also great for our physical health too.

A 2009 study of over 73,000 Japanese men and women found that those who had a strong connection to their sense of purpose tended to live longer than those who didn't. Dr Patricia Boyle, a neuropsychologist at the RUSH Alzheimers Center in Chicago, also found that people with a low sense of purpose were 2.4 times more likely to get Alzheimers than those with a strong purpose.

***

In summary, then, research suggests that people who have a deep sense of purpose, strong values and a passion in life are healthier, more resilient, happier and more in control of their lives. They also experience less stress, anxiety and fewer bouts of depression.

We need purpose, values and passion in life just like we need to feel like we belong and connect to others, because we need to feel like we are adding value. Knowing your purpose will help guide how you choose to live your life and what you choose to strive for over other things. In short, having purpose connects us to ourselves. And when you feel connected to yourself, you will grow in strength.

REAL PEOPLE

"Falling ill led me to take the plunge and follow my dream." – Lisa

Lisa Dalgarno-Connelly, on finding her 'ultimate concern' and fulfilling her lifelong dream.

'I'd been a teacher for 24 years when I was signed off with stress last year. I just couldn't understand it. I've always thought of myself as such a strong person. I had coped with really stressful jobs as an assistant head before, and although I was only doing maternity cover now, I was falling apart. I just couldn't cope with the workload, in particular the constant scrutiny by management of book-marking. Nothing I did was ever enough. I started to have panic attacks in the shower at the thought of going to work. I'd be ok in front of the children, but it got to the point where I couldn't trust my own body. What if I started sweating and shaking when I was teaching? I felt like a complete failure.

Eventually, I thought: there has to be more to life than this – marking was taking over what little free time I had to spend with my own children – I just wasn't sure what that was, or what I wanted to do instead. I was signed off in May and then that summer, my husband (who is also a teacher) and I went on holiday. The break and change of scenery gave us the chance to really think about what our purpose was in life. It helped us to revisit a dream we'd always had, which was to open a bar together. There was just never the right time. The kids were too young, or we didn't feel we could take the risk of giving up our steady income to work for ourselves. But the more we thought about it, the more we realized that it had to be now or never: we're both passionate about live music and love bar culture –
so why not take this opportunity to turn that into our jobs? It would be hard work, but we knew that doing something we were passionate about would make it worth it.

We broke the whole thing down into little goals, so it felt more manageable. We made a business plan – or a plan of what sort of bar we wanted it to be – then we found a building in our local area. It was perfect, so we put in a bid. We won, and now it's being made into our dream bar.

It's scary, because both of us were on a stable wage and this feels risky. I was also floored by what happened to me and lost a lot of confidence, so meeting builders and so on has felt even more out of my comfort zone, but because it's what I really want to do, I'm determined to make it work. Making myself do this stuff has given me my confidence back and I realize I always had that resilience in me, I just had to find it again.

It's a shame it took me getting ill for us to change our lives, but looking on the bright side, it's meant that I have questioned and then found my purpose, so maybe it was meant to happen. I see that so many people stay in the status quo because it's all they've ever done and it's safe, but it's important to question that sometimes – *why* am I doing this – is it what I want to do? What have I got to lose if I try something else?

Opening a bar is scary but it feels nowhere near as scary as going to work as a teacher every day. It was like we dared to step out of our comfort zone, thought about what we really wanted and then went for it – and the stars all aligned. Now we've taken the plunge, failure is not an option! As my motto goes: Everything will be alright in the end, and if it's not okay, it's not the end yet!'

HOW RESILIENT ARE YOU?

Resilience is the 'bounce-back' factor, your inner store of personal grit that you can call on when the going gets tough. It's one of those qualities that we tend to take for granted and only notice when it lets us down. But resilience is quietly operating on a daily basis, helping you to keep going by ensuring that minor challenges and disappointments don't turn into crises. What supports and what undermines it is different for everyone – you might feel more resilient when you pay attention to your personal wellbeing, when you feel supported by your relationships or you have a sense of purpose. For others, it's connected to self-confidence and self-belief. Becoming aware of what supports and what undermines your personal resilience is the key to protecting it and helping it flourish.

Test by Sally Brown

QUESTION 1

You have a big job interview coming up. Your priority the night before is to:

A. Work out if the job is really what you want.
B. Get a good night's sleep.
C. Talk through potential questions and answers with a friend.
D. Remind yourself of what you can bring to the role.

QUESTION 2

Your ideal holiday involves:

A. Exercising, eating well, and winding down.
B. Spending time with people you care about.
C. Challenging yourself or trying something new.
D. Exploring a new culture or volunteering.

QUESTION 3

Staying upbeat feels harder when you're:

A. Away from home.
B. Out of your comfort zone.
C. Doing something mundane.
D. Tired or under the weather.

QUESTION 4

Life is going well when you feel:

A. Comfortable in your own skin.
B. Optimistic about the future.
C. Focused and full of energy.
D. Part of a community.

QUESTION 5

You get a buzz from:

A. Making a difference.
B. Pushing yourself physically.
C. Helping other people.
D. Getting positive feedback.

QUESTION 6

You know you've taken on too much when you:

A. Catch every bug going.
B. Feel like cancelling social events.
C. Worry about little things.
D. Wonder what it's all about.

QUESTION 7

Looking back, you've got through tough times in the past by:

A. Leaning on your friends.
B. Believing in yourself.
C. Thinking big picture.
D. Looking after yourself.

QUESTION 8

When you wake up in the middle of the night, you're most likely to worry about:

A. Being out of your depth.
B. People you care about.
C. Your health or weight.
D. Past decisions.

QUESTION 9

Which of these would be the best investment in yourself?

A. A course of counselling or psychotherapy.
B. Personal training or a consultation with a nutritionist.
C. A series of life coaching sessions.
D. A confidence building or personal empowerment workshop.

QUESTION 10

Overcoming adversity in the past has taught you:

A. The value of looking after your health.
B. The importance of good relationships.
C. That you have to believe in yourself.
D. To be guided by your values.

Now add up your scores from each answer, and find out what underpins your personal resilience, using the following table.

	A	B	C	D
Q1	2	4	6	8
Q2	4	6	8	2
Q3	6	8	2	4
Q4	8	2	4	6
Q5	2	4	6	8
Q6	4	6	8	2
Q7	6	8	2	4
Q8	8	2	4	6
Q9	2	4	6	8
Q10	4	6	8	2

If you scored between 20 and 35 ...

Your resilience is linked to a sense of purpose

Staying in touch with what matters to you, and living a life that is in line with your values, determines how well you deal with setbacks and challenges. You naturally think big picture, and if you lose that sense of purpose, life can feel like a grind and your resilience is affected. Your resilience is compromised as soon as you feel that you are not living authentically. What is key for you is doing work that engages you, and making sure you spend quality time with people you connect with.

If you scored between 36 and 45 ...
Your resilience is linked to your physical wellbeing

The mind and body link is key for you, and when you feel physically strong you also feel mentally resilient. Your mindset reflects your energy and your moods are a barometer of your wellbeing. When you feel well, you have a naturally optimistic outlook and can positively re-frame most situations. But when you feel tired, or you neglect your self-care, your mood and outlook tend to dip. You need to check in with yourself every day, and ask: 'How am I feeling? What do I need to feel my best today?'

If you scored between 46 and 60 ...
Your resilience is linked to your relationships

Social support improves resilience in most people, but for you, it's the key factor. When you feel supported and understood by people who you care about, you feel like you can deal with most things. You are a natural team player at work and often find yourself mentoring and supporting others. Your resilience is compromised when you feel unsupported, so you struggle more than most to get over break-ups or deal with conflict at work. But rather than ruminating, talking through your problems will help you process them and find a solution.

If you scored between 61 and 80 ...
Your resilience is linked to your self-belief

When your self-confidence is low, you feel buffeted by the storms of life. Minor problems feel like huge hurdles, and small disagreements can seem like major sources of conflict. You may have always struggled with self-esteem and, even if you have worked hard to change the way you feel about yourself, it remains your weak point. The first sign for you that your resilience is low is being self-critical or doubting of yourself. It's time to start treating yourself like your own best friend.

CHAPTER 5

TACKLING CHANGE

Chances are you're going through a period of great change in your life right now. Change is one thing we can rely on happening, and yet many of us find it hard to navigate. Big changes in life – and small ones – can make us feel destabilized and anxious about the unknown on the other side. Change means uncertainty and stepping out of our comfort zone, and so it tests our resilience. In fact, the quickest and easiest way to measure your inner resilience is to observe your own reactions and behaviour as you experience change. Some people are naturally change-averse and some people relish it. There are probably more people in the first camp than the latter, but one thing's for sure, change WILL happen and tackling it well is at the heart of real strength.

The good news is there are plenty of techniques you can learn to help you to do that. We'll be exploring them in this chapter.

WE'RE WIRED FOR CHANGE – WE NEED IT FOR GROWTH

If you feel like you're struggling through whatever change you're going through, it may be comforting to bear in mind that, as human beings, it's something we need.

In fact, as tricky and scary as it can sometimes feel, we cannot grow or develop without it. Change is necessary for human accomplishment – it is at the heart of our own life stories, and of the stories we read. The reason we read and enjoy fiction is because we see the characters undergoing transformation. They do this by experiencing struggle. You know that satisfying feeling you get at the end of a good book when you feel like you've witnessed the hero go through hell and come out the other side? That's no accident. That process is the basis for all narratives and the basis for *our* stories of growth too.

The American mythologist Joseph Campbell coined the phrase the 'hero's journey' to describe this path of change and development. The hero's journey has five specific stages. We go through these same stages when we ourselves go through changes in our lives:

1. **Old status quo:** This is the starting point to our stories of thriving after adversity. It's where we are before the change.
2. **Destabilizing events:** These are anything that thrust us forwards into big life changes; for example, being fired, or even something like becoming a parent (especially if it was unplanned).
3. **Crucible of change:** This is the point at which the character (you) comes into contact with the big obstacle or challenge you have to get over in order to come out the other side, a changed person.
4. **Integration practice:** This is where we accept whatever changes have happened to us and deal with the outcome and changes in our circumstances. We adapt and try to grow and thrive, because of and despite it.
5. **New status quo:** Our new life and the new us, post change.

WHY IS CHANGE SO STRESSFUL?

> **"A huge amount of upheaval may well cause anxiety, especially if we don't understand why the change is happening."**
>
> Liggy Webb, consultant in behavioural skills and author of *Resilience*

One of the main reasons that change is so stressful, and why it can stop you feeling strong and resilient, is that it threatens your perceived sense of control. This happens even with change that we want – such as moving house or finding a new relationship – but it is especially true of sudden and traumatic change: someone close to us becoming seriously ill, for example. It's really difficult to think calmly and rationally when change is thrust upon us like this because everything seems so surreal – so out of our control.

> 66 **Everything outside your world looks distant and alien. The normality of life shifts so dramatically that it seems as though you can't ever access it again.** 99
>
> Sian Williams, author of *RISE: Surviving and Thriving After Trauma*

This feeling – that we have lost control – is perfectly natural. We are creatures of habit, after all, and generally feel safer when things are familiar – be that our job, relationship or home. Put another way, when things change, we can feel unsafe, stressed out and frightened – the very opposite of real strength.

In the 1960s, the Swiss-American psychiatrist Elisabeth Kubler-Ross developed the 'grief cycle model'. She proposed that any terminally ill patient would go through these five stages of grief on learning they were going to die. She also proposed that this model could be applied to anyone going through any life-changing situation – that is, any big change. It makes sense, since if you think about it, change IS loss: instead of losing a loved one, you are losing things being the way they were, so it's no wonder it can throw us off course.

Take a look at them. Do you recognize any of the stages in terms of how you feel or have felt when going through change in your life?

1. **Denial:** This is the stage where whatever change you are going through is so overwhelming that you don't want to believe or accept that it's really happening; where you might even not want to discuss it with anyone.
2. **Anger:** You might lash out with the stress of it all – depending on what the change is, you might be angrily asking: why me? What have I done to deserve this?
3. **Bargaining:** This is the stage where you question the looming change itself, either with other people or within yourself: is this the right thing to be doing? If I did such and such, might I not have to go through with it at all?
4. **Depression:** You might feel sadness at things changing; after all you are waving goodbye to things being a certain way – a way you have felt comfortable with – and have no idea what things will be like after the change.
5. **Acceptance:** This is the last stage of grief. It's not about feeling happy (although, you *may* feel happy); it's more a stage of calm, a feeling that you have made peace with whatever change you're going through and have grown as a person because of it. This is the stage where you are most likely to find the positives and the benefits of that change in circumstances, even if it felt very stressful while you were going through it.

Not all people will experience all of these stages when going through big changes in their lives, and you may find you get stuck on one stage – for example, denial. However, by understanding each stage of Kubler-Ross's grief cycle model, we can better understand how to tackle the process of change. By recognizing and being aware of your behaviour in each stage, you can learn how to get to the acceptance part quicker and start to enjoy and embrace the outcome of the change that has taken place.

❝Resilient people know that things change. They accept that it's part of life and they get to the 'acceptance' bit a lot sooner. ❞

Liggy Webb, consultant in behavioural skills and author of *Resilience*

ASK YOURSELF

Ⓠ What is it specifically about the change you're going through that you're finding stressful? Identify those things and the feelings around them. For example, is it the uncertainty you're most stressed about? How is that making you feel?

Ⓠ Is there anything about your situation that you CAN control? (Remember – control the controllable!)

Ⓠ Do you recognize yourself in any of the grief cycle stages? Could you possibly be stuck at any of them?

IT'S THE TRANSITION, NOT NECESSARILY THE CHANGE, THAT'S HARD

'It isn't the changes that do you in, it's the transitions', says William Bridges, author of *Managing Transition*. Transition, in this sense, means the psychological process people must go through to come to terms with new situations. There are two main bits to this process:

1. Accepting the change (see the last stage of the grief cycle).
2. Knowing how to consciously direct your life towards something more positive.

We'll be looking at how to do that, in more detail, in a second.

PERCEPTION IS EVERYTHING

Just as people's coping strategies differ when faced with adversity and change, so do their *perceptions* of that change and adversity. You may think that some changes in life would be seen as traumatic by everybody – being diagnosed with an incurable illness for example – but actually, that's not the case. So what does someone who *doesn't* perceive a terminal illness diagnosis as 'traumatic' have to teach us? How come they're so strong?

In her book *RISE: Surviving and Thriving After Trauma*, Sian Williams tells the story of her brother-in-law Martin who has stage four, incurable cancer but who does not see this as 'traumatic'. Yes, he hates the chemotherapy and how the illness limits his life. He also recognizes that he's had to make certain amendments to his life as a result of the diagnosis, but he doesn't view these as traumatic either.

So what does Martin do? What is it about his thinking that means he does not perceive this seismic shift to his life as traumatic?

* He reflects. He discusses his condition with his wife and family and does not pretend that it's not happening.
* He researches and embraces alternative therapies.
* He is active and proactive, rather than in denial, and takes control of the things he can manage. For example, he's stopped eating sugar as he thinks it's toxic, and he stopped chemo for a while when he felt it was limiting his life.

We could encapsulate his approach like this:

Martin cannot control this cancer, so he is actively thinking about how to integrate it into a fulfilling life. He is reflecting about his predicament. Also, he is exerting control where he can at the same time as being flexible and adaptable.

As Williams writes:

> *'Martin is not stuck in a loop of why me? He's thinking, ok there's no cure for this so what can I do to make my life more bearable, even enjoyable? If we can all do that, then we can build up resilience.'*

TACKLING UNCERTAINTY

It's very probable that if you're going through big changes in your life, it's the fear of uncertainty that is causing the most anxiety. As human beings we have to deal with uncertainty every day. We have to manage the state of not knowing as our lives are filled with unexpected events and surprises, but this is how we grow and progress in life. A certain amount of fear of what may lie ahead is natural, but if it is paralysing you, stopping you from living the life you want to live … you need to look at it.

Researchers Michel Dugas and Robert Ladouceur found that a core feature of worry is the inability to tolerate uncertainty. They found that some worriers even say that they would rather know for certain that the outcome will be bad, than be left in suspense over whether things will work out or not.

Perhaps it is worth pointing out here that since we can *never* know what lies in the future, worrying about it is not only a colossal waste of energy but also perpetuates stress. So how do we deal with it?

The trick is to practise sitting with our feelings of discomfort as we experience fear of uncertainty. Sufferers tend to try and second guess everything, so instead, try and trust your instincts and judgement. If something feels truly wrong, then it's possibly because it is, and fear of uncertainty can sometimes be our brain's way of protecting us from things that are bad for us (for example, a bad relationship). On the flipside, if we have too much unchecked fear, it can stop us from taking opportunities because we worry they won't work out. So get curious about your fears: what are they really about? Are you worrying about something that is merely hypothetical? For example, that this person will get cold feet and hurt you? You can manage fears like this by enforcing boundaries: say to yourself (in the case of beginning a new relationship, just as an example) 'I will treat this relationship as a certainty for 30 days and not worry about the outcome. At the end of those 30 days, I shall reassess my feelings: has what I was worried about materialized?'

ASK YOURSELF

Q Are you scared of the uncertainty with regards to the outcome of your situation?

Q How could you compartmentalize your fears to make it easier? Could you put a boundary around them? 'I will put on hold worrying about this for a week, then reassess', for example.

MAINTAINING REAL STRENGTH IN THE FACE OF CHANGE

We are all resilient creatures. But how can we access our well of resiliency, even at times of catastrophic change?

1. **Be self-aware:** As with everything to do with building real strength, knowing yourself is the first step. Only you can

go through this change, so knowing how you tend to react to change is vital. Once you are aware of how you tend to think in times of change and stress, you can challenge that thinking if it's not helpful. You can separate your thoughts from yourself, rather than letting your thoughts spiral. Simply saying '*I am having the thought that ...*' helps you separate your thought from whatever you are going through, reducing your anxiety.

2. **Ask for support:** There is a lot to be said for the old adage: a problem shared is a problem halved. Seeking the support of others, especially those who have been through or are going through the same thing as you, can be incredibly comforting and bolstering. Resilient people surround themselves with support from trusted friends and family because they understand the value that has. Not only does knowing you are loved and cherished when going through a hard time help enormously, but hearing how other people have dealt with a similar problem can give you ideas as to how you can do the same.

3. **Reflect:** As in the case of Martin who reflected about his cancer diagnosis, putting time aside to think about your predicament is the first step in healthily tackling it. Reflection is perhaps the opposite of reaction. As we saw in Part 1, when we are in reflection mode, we activate our frontal cortex – the part of our brain that helps us to make sound decisions and to rationalize – and this automatically reduces activity in the amygdala which activates our stress response and often leads us to doing and saying things we may later regret.

4. **Be flexible:** Flexible people are adaptable when responding to uncertainty – they are able to identify and compartmentalize their fears about the future. They recognize that worrying about something that may not happen is not a good use of their energy, and so they are able to put those fears in a

box in order to continue with their lives. They are also able to see fears for what they are – FEARS, ideas – not realities or facts. Another prerequisite for flexible thinking is being open to other peoples' suggestions on how best to tackle a challenge.

5. **Accept it might be messy:** It probably will be! This is because going through big changes forces us to reassess and scrutinize belief systems we have upheld all our lives – it can feel like our whole universe is shifting on its axis. But just because things feel messy, doesn't mean you're not growing as a person.

GET A DIFFERENT PERSPECTIVE ON THINGS

Identify someone who typically approaches things differently than you do and ask them for input on a particularly difficult aspect of your change initiative – listen to their ideas without interrupting or passing judgement.

As we already touched upon briefly in Part 1, in her book *RISE: Surviving and Thriving After Trauma*, Sian Williams introduces us to Professor Stephen Joseph, who has worked with survivors of adversity for more than 20 years. Professor Joseph told Williams the story of American psychologist Carl Rogers, and Williams then regaled the tale in her book. As a boy living on a ranch outside Chicago, Rogers would go down to the cellar where his family stored potatoes. The ceiling of the cellar was made of solid wood but there was a small gap, and the sprouts of the potatoes would always find a way to grow towards it – they would seek the light.

Professor Joseph likens this to the 'self-actualizing tendency' in human beings.

We, too, will always find a way to grow even in very difficult circumstances. But just like those potatoes, which were gnarled and grey, we may appear and feel unhealthy as we do it. Basically, change means struggle, and struggle can be ugly. However, Professor Joseph's time spent with individuals going through trauma has taught him that just because a person may look like they are struggling, it doesn't mean they are not growing inside. He says: 'Like the shoots reaching out in the darkness, the potato looks very unhealthy ... and if you looked at a person who was similarly trying to grow, you may not see lots of lovely positive things – it may look quite nasty, but it would still be that person striving to grow.'

LIGGY WEBB'S TEN-POINT CHECKLIST FOR MANAGING CHANGE

1. *'Reassure yourself that just because some things are changing, not everything is, so try your best to keep as many familiar things around you as possible as a reminder of what's stable in your life.*
2. *Stick to normal routines and see people you normally see.*
3. *Be proactive, not reactive: this means engaging with the change rather than fighting against it. Think about it in terms of taking 'offence' in response to the change, rather than 'defence'.*
4. *Practise calculating risks and applying lessons from past experiences to similar challenges you have faced. Make a list of the pros and cons to different outcomes, asking yourself: 'what if?'*
5. *Develop plans for worst-case scenarios.*

6. *Ask yourself how much you can control – then assert that control.*
7. *Celebrate the positives – what lessons can you take from this experience?*
8. *Take responsibility for your reactions and choices. The antidote to negativity and pessimism is to learn to accept responsibility for your situation. The very act of responsibility cancels out any negative emotion and lays the foundations for self-respect and pride.*
9. *Have hope for the future.*
10. *Remember: you will grow as a person, but you will be still the same at your core.'*

ASK YOURSELF

Q What is the 'change' you are going through at the moment in terms of the actual event? So a divorce, a redundancy, the children having left home or whatever.

Q What is the *transition* you are going through? For example (in the case of the children leaving home), being used to family meals and having people to look after, to not feeling 'needed'. Making the differentiation between 'change' and 'transition' is a very important part of understanding your struggle – why you feel the way you do.

Q What things about your situation are going to stay the same?

Q Even though you cannot control the outcome of this period of transition, what things can you control? (Hint: the way you respond to it for starters.)

HOW DO YOU REACT TO UNCERTAINTY?

As humans, we have a paradoxical relationship to change, craving it and dreading it in equal measures. However much your logical mind may embrace the need for change and welcome the opportunity to grow, the more primitive, emotional part of your brain can interpret uncertainty as danger. But we face uncertainty in all areas of life, from not knowing what people think of us or how we are perceived in a social or work situation, to uncertainty over a specific outcome – like an exam result or health investigation. Logical as it may seem, the solution is not to eliminate uncertainty in life, as the effort involved in doing so ultimately creates more difficulties. By developing our tolerance of uncertainty, we can develop our resilience, with a knock-on effect on our happiness levels. The first step is to identify your current approach to change, so you can see if it's helping or undermining your ability to deal with uncertainty.

Test by Sally Brown

QUESTION 1

A good friend invites you to a party where you won't know anyone but the host. Your immediate reaction is to:

A. Feel anxious and think of excuses not to go.
B. Think of who you can get to go with you.
C. Wonder if you could go and leave after an hour.
D. Not want to go, then feel guilty for letting your friend down.

QUESTION 2

On your way to an important meeting, you get stuck in a traffic jam. You react by:

A. Phoning your best friend or partner to rant.
B. Feeling fairly calm because you left extra early.
C. Berating yourself for not leaving earlier.
D. Feeling anxious and stressed.

QUESTION 3

Your new boss at work seems inscrutable and inapproachable. What internal dialogue does it trigger?

A. 'Keep your head down, look busy and keep quiet.'
B. 'Don't mess this up, you have to make a good impression.'
C. 'I'm bound to get sacked so I need to start looking for a new job.'
D. 'I wonder what everyone else thinks?'

QUESTION 4

In the early days of a new relationship, you tend to feel:

A. Determined not to mess it up.
B. Happy in an anxious sort of way.
C. Raw and in touch with your emotions.
D. Wary and self-protective.

QUESTION 5

Conflict in a close relationship makes you feel:

A. Stressed and worried.

B. Attacked and alone.

C. Like distancing yourself emotionally.

D. As if you've done something wrong.

QUESTION 6

The first sign that you're feeling uncertain is:

A. Not wanting to be on your own.

B. Procrastinating and avoiding making decisions.

C. Questioning yourself and feeling self-critical.

D. Your stress levels going up.

QUESTION 7

Facing change is always easier when you:

A. Have time to research your options.

B. Feel self-confident.

C. Feel calm and relaxed.

D. Have enough support.

QUESTION 8

You admire people who appear to have great:

A. Self-belief.

B. Courage.

C. Resilience.

D. Inner calm.

QUESTION 9

If you could make one change, you would:

A. Get less stressed about what might happen.

B. Be less affected by other people's moods.

C. Be braver and say yes to the opportunities you're offered.

D. Have more confidence and belief in what you're capable of.

QUESTION 10

You have a big deadline but can't seem to focus. What's going through your mind?

A. 'Why does this always happen to me?'

B. 'I should have started much earlier.'

C. 'You are such an idiot.'

D. 'I can't cope with this stress.'

Now add up your scores from each answer, and find out how you react to uncertainty, using the following table:

	A	B	C	D
Q1	2	4	6	8
Q2	4	6	8	2
Q3	6	8	2	4
Q4	8	2	4	6
Q5	2	4	6	8
Q6	4	6	8	2
Q7	6	8	2	4
Q8	8	2	4	6
Q9	2	4	6	8
Q10	4	6	8	2

If you scored between 20 and 35 ...

Uncertainty makes you anxious

As a creative thinker, you have an active imagination, but the downside is that you can vividly picture everything that could possibly go wrong. If you allow yourself to ruminate, you can also convince yourself that your worst-case scenario fantasies are actually real. The knock-on effect can increase your stress and anxiety levels. Mindfulness can help you rein in your imagination – when you feel your anxiety levels rising, try using your breath as an anchor for your mind, or simply grounding yourself in the present moment by checking in with what you are hearing, smelling or seeing.

If you scored between 36 and 45 ...
Uncertainty makes you feel vulnerable

Not knowing the outcome of a situation, or what is expected of you, can erode your self-confidence, so even if you're normally self-sufficient, you may find yourself needing reassurance from others. You may become more sensitive to criticism than usual as you look to others for validation that you're doing OK. Spending time with supportive people is crucial for you during times of uncertainty. Remind yourself that experiencing uncertainty can ultimately make us stronger, showing us that we can get through difficult times and learn from them.

If you scored between 46 and 60 ...
Uncertainty makes you cautious

It's not surprising that uncertainty makes us cautious – it kept our evolutionary ancestors alive. But being too cautious can put the brakes on your life. When you are operating from a place of caution, you can find it hard to make decisions (in case you get it wrong), so you find yourself procrastinating. You may also find yourself trying to exert control by micro-managing situations, or becoming black and white in your views and opinions. Try arming yourself with knowledge instead, replacing imagined threats with facts or opinion, giving you an informed standpoint from which to act.

If you scored between 61 and 80 ...
Uncertainty makes you self-critical

You may have perfectionist tendencies and are secretly convinced that being hard on yourself is what keeps you achieving. You find it hard to accept that you find uncertainty challenging because it can seem like a weakness or failing. Perhaps you internalized a critical parental voice during your childhood, which may manifest as seemingly innocuous thoughts such as, 'Don't mess this up!', or be more obviously undermining, calling yourself names for not being able to cope. The truth is that you need self-compassion not self-criticism when you're dealing with uncertainty. Try experimenting with giving yourself encouragement, and being your own coach, then notice the difference it makes to how you feel emotionally.

CHAPTER 6

STRENGTH ROBBERS

There's no doubt about it that remaining strong, as well as thriving after adversity, is no mean feat. It's a journey rather than a destination, however, and like all cognitive and psychological journeys, you can smooth the way with good preparation and arm yourself with knowledge. There is also an awful lot you can do to help yourself – and knowing and pre-empting pitfalls is a fantastic way to begin! There are certain mindsets and bad habits you can watch out for to give yourself a head start. In this chapter, we explore them.

1. CHASING PERFECTION

The problem with perfectionism is that perfection does not exist. For this reason, chasing it is not only a waste of energy but is going to make you feel less robust, not more so. Not only will it make you feel like you are constantly failing (because you can never succeed in attaining something that doesn't exist), but like you never even got started.

Perfectionism can take many forms: you may, for example, really want to be in a relationship, but say to yourself that only Mr/Mrs Perfect will do. From this standpoint you can't accept compromise, and as a consequence it's going to be very difficult to meet anybody. Perhaps you've always had in your head the 'perfect' life of that amazing partner, two children (one of each), big house, fantastic holidays. But then life throws you a curveball: an injury forces you to rethink your career or your partner develops depression. Perfectionists will struggle: how can I go forward with this less-than-perfect life?

In this way, we can see how seeking perfection keeps us in a state of paralysis, the very opposite of real strength which is about growth and progression. Perfectionists might seem like productive characters, but sometimes in the pursuit of perfection you can fail to fulfil your potential. This is because you're too scared to give things a go in case you're not good enough. We know from Part 1 that failing is a crucial part of building resilience, so we can see the problem this presents!

> **"Gritty people don't seek perfection, but instead strive for excellence ... Perfection is someone else's perception of an ideal and pursuing it is like chasing a hallucination."**
>
> Angela Duckworth, author of *Grit*

ASK YOURSELF

Ⓠ Do you sometimes not attempt things because you're worried you won't be able to do them to a high enough standard?

Ⓠ Take one thing in your life where you feel you won't settle for less than perfect (finding a partner, the cleanliness of your home) and write a list: things I could compromise on, things I can't compromise on. Try to make them equal! Think about what 'good enough' constitutes for you.

2. BEING A CATASTROPHIST

> **"What can you control about this situation? You can control how you respond to it."**
>
> Liggy Webb, consultant in behavioural skills and author of *Resilience*

'Catastrophist' comes from the word 'catastrophe' and describes people who have a tendency to see everything that happens to them either as a catastrophe or a potential one! You know the type who always thinks in terms of 'worst-case scenario'? For example, 'We're going to miss the flight, and if we *do* miss the flight then we'll *never* get another one!', or dramatize situations by exclaiming 'This is a *total nightmare*!' Catastrophists are a fan of absolutes, so their self-talk tends to be full of the words 'never' and 'always': 'I'm *always* missing trains'; 'I'm *never* going to meet anyone'; 'I'm *always* getting let down by people'. Where managing adversity is concerned, the problem with living very much in a black and white world is that life *isn't* black and white. Life is full of grey areas; of possibilities and alternatives. Resilient people are able to rise above their worries and see these, and if they can't see them, they're able to find them.

The other problem with catastrophizing self-talk is that you begin to believe your own hype. So what to someone else might seem like just a minor hitch – to the catastrophist is, well, a catastrophe! This is because they're telling themselves 'this is the worst thing that's ever happened to anyone'. So they begin to feel it.

Catastrophizing also limits our ability to bounce back because it's a way of shirking responsibility. If we put ourselves in the eye of a self-made storm, then we can put off having to deal with that storm or taking responsibility for it. We're having a nightmare! Of course we can't sit down and be strategic! Often, when we say, 'It's so unfair, I'm always missing trains' what we actually mean is, 'I'm so annoyed with myself. I need to leave more time.' The interesting thing about this is that when we eventually take responsibility for a situation, rather than catastrophize over it, we feel better, because we're in a place of acceptance rather than fighting it – and it's only when we've accepted something that we can work to find a way out of it.

ASK YOURSELF

 When you look back, are things often not as bad as you thought they were in the moment? Next time you find yourself in a less-than-ideal situation, write down what the situation was and how you felt about it immediately after it happened. Revisit it, an hour and then a day later – does it seem as bad now?

Be honest with yourself: do you sometimes catastrophize what's going on, because the alternative – of saying to yourself, 'I messed up', or 'it's my fault I missed my train because I didn't get up early enough' – is harder to do?

What steps could you take to prevent it happening next time?

HUNT OUT THE GOOD STUFF

When something bad happens to you, look at the worst-case scenario, then the best-case scenario, then write down one good thing that can come out of the experience – because there's always *something*. You just have to find it.

3. DWELLING AND RUMINATION

We learnt in Chapter 2 that rumination is basically trying to problem solve. It's either worrying about the future: 'how will I cope if things don't get better?' Or regretfully focusing on the past: 'why did I let this happen to me? Why am I such an idiot?' We are fooled into thinking that worrying and ruminating is productive, because we are thinking about the problem, but it can become circular – we aren't going anywhere psychologically and so it undermines our resilience and confidence and often leaves us feeling more vulnerable, stuck and helpless.

When it comes to rising above adversity, the only place we can make changes is in the present. Mindfulness practice can help bring our attention and focus to the present moment, thus opening up a calm space for us to form a perspective on our ever-changing thoughts and feelings. So, instead of being pushed around by them, we are able to observe them and notice them calmly. From this vantage point, we have greater choice about whether or not to engage with certain thoughts.

When we are practising mindfulness, we are also reducing activity in the amygdala, the part of the brain that turns on our stress response in the face of perceived threat and danger. When the amygdala is activated, we switch into 'doing mode', trying to take action against the stressful situation, which often involves engaging in lots of worry and rumination. In 'doing mode' we lose our ability to think rationally and often make knee-jerk decisions. Mindfulness, on the other hand, helps us to turn on our 'being mode' – in this mode we are able to think more clearly and function better while we make wiser choices about how to respond to and improve the situation.

DR MICHAEL SINCLAIR ON USING MINDFULNESS TO BUILD INNER STRENGTH

'Mindfulness practice is all about bringing your attention away from thoughts about the past or the future (where we can't do anything) and back to the present moment. It's not about clearing your mind of thoughts, trying to distract yourself *from them, or suppressing any painful feelings. Instead, it's about noticing your present moment experience, including any thoughts and feelings as they arise, moment by moment.*

Bring your awareness to your sensory experience in that moment: what can you smell? Hear? Feel? It might be as simple as noticing body sensations – your back against the chair, your feet on the floor. Purposely increasing physical sensation in the here and now can help to bring us back to the moment. So, bring your fingers together, push your fingertips against each other and release them – do that a few times and notice the changing sensations in your hands. (I call them spider press-ups.) Or we can push our feet into the floor a couple of times.

It's all about bringing our attention to our experience in the here and now, allowing any thoughts and feelings to come and go, rise and fall, as they naturally will. If your mind wanders off and becomes caught up in the content of thoughts again, that is absolutely fine and just what the human mind does. If you notice these distractions, well done, great noticing! That is what mindfulness practice is all about, and you've just unhooked yourself again with present moment awareness. Now, just gently escort your attention back to your sensory experience.

Another way we can do this is by noticing our breath: notice the difference in temperature as we draw breath in and then breathe out; the sensation in the nostrils, the rhythm and movement of our chest and stomach rising on the in-breath and falling again on each out-breath. Be in the moment, noticing these things for five or so minutes.

As you cultivate more present moment awareness, letting thoughts and feelings go by, like clouds passing in the sky, you may notice how you start to feel calmer, and experience a sense of inner strength and serenity even in the presence of any distressing thoughts and feelings.'

These techniques are not designed to get rid of worrying or ruminating – the only agenda is being in the presence of your active mind rather than becoming caught up in it; to notice it at work, moment by moment. Don't panic if you're pulled back into worry or rumination – if this happens (which is only natural and what the human mind does), just notice this distraction again, perhaps congratulate yourself for noticing it (as that's what mindfulness is), and then gently guide your attention back to the present moment, by tuning into your sensory experience to help ground you back into the here and now once again.

ASK YOURSELF

Ⓠ Do I tend to live in the past or the future? Worrying about things that have already happened, or what might happen?

Ⓠ Does this change anything?

Ⓠ Could I commit to five minutes a day of mindfulness practice – using the techniques above?

4. VICTIM MENTALITY

It's very tempting, when something bad happens, to fall into the 'poor me' trap. Victim mentality behaviour can take many forms:

- You might complain incessantly to people.
- You become a martyr ('no, it's ok, I can cope. Don't worry about me!').
- You exaggerate your problems, making out they are bigger than anyone else's.

It's perfectly natural to feel sorry for ourselves when going through a tough time. The trick is to avoid staying in that state for too long. It's a position of powerlessness, and so the longer you stay in the 'poor me' space, the longer you put off doing anything about it.

"People with a victim mentality get into a vicious circle: they convince themselves there's no point in doing anything about their situation because nothing will come of it – it's 'learned helplessness.'"

Amy Morin, psychotherapist and author of *13 Things Mentally Strong People Don't Do*

HOW IS LEARNED HELPLESSNESS A BARRIER TO REAL STRENGTH?

In order to understand what 'learned helplessness' is exactly, let's turn to the study which led to the term being coined. In 1965, as part of his work trying to better understand depression, the psychologist Martin Seligman conducted an experiment: he rang a bell and then gave a dog a light shock.

After a number of repetitions, the dog reacted to the shock even before it happened: as soon as the dog heard the bell, he reacted as though he'd already been shocked. Then Seligman put each dog into a large crate that was divided down the middle with a low fence. The dog could see and jump over the fence if necessary.

The floor on one side of the fence was electrified, but not on the other side. Seligman put the dog on the electrified side and administered a light shock. He expected the dog to jump to the non-shocking side, but instead, the dog lay down. It was as though he'd learned from the first part of the experiment that there was nothing he could do to avoid the shocks, so he gave up in the second part of the experiment; whereas dogs that had not taken part in the first experiment DID jump the fence.

Seligman called this behaviour 'learned helplessness'– and it's something that, as humans, we are also prone to. Not doing anything to help yourself in an adverse situation, because past experience has told you there's no point, is learned helplessness. It's accepting loss of power and control over the situation and it's what happens when we succumb to a victim mentality. It doesn't do us much harm to succumb now and again, but psychologists have found that persistent learned helplessness (and victim mentality) – believing that we have no control over the outcome of situations – is a leading cause of depression.

Interestingly, the way we view negative events that happen to us has a big impact on *whether* we feel helpless or not. Psychologists call these ways of thinking 'attributions' and they have found that certain types of attributions cause learned helplessness. These are:

- **Internal attribution:** Perceiving that the cause of the negative event is within YOU. *I didn't get the job because I am stupid.*
- **Stable attribution:** Believing that this cause is a permanent state. *I didn't get the job because I am stupid.*
- **Global attribution:** The belief that the factors affecting the outcome apply to a large number of situations not just one of them. *I didn't get the job because I am stupid just like I failed my driving test because I am stupid.*

It follows, then, that if learned helplessness and victim mentality are caused by these ways of thinking, if we can challenge our thinking and change it, then we will not fall prey to either.

AMY MORIN ON HOW TO GET OUT OF A VICTIM MENTALITY

- *'Curb the complaining. The more time and energy we spend complaining, the less we are doing to sort the situation – it's just offloading.*

- *Learn to distinguish between different ways of thinking. Are you just re-hashing things over and over again? Either in your own head (ruminating) or to others (whining). Or is this problem-solving type thinking, which is progressive and about solutions not symptoms. Catch yourself if it's the former and think: what one positive step can I take to make my life better right now?*

- *Behave contrary to how you feel: you might feel low and badly done to, but if you make yourself get up and do something positive and hopeful, you may well end up feeling the same way.*

- *Try not to think in black and white. Curb your use of words like 'always' and 'never' and try to see any challenging situations as the isolated situations they are, rather than a general reflection of your life (i.e. I didn't get this promotion, but there will be other opportunities).'*

5. LETTING STRESS GET TO YOU

Stress is, of course, a huge subject and compromises our inner strength in many different ways. There are also different kinds of stress – short-term, chronic, toxic – there is even 'good' stress, if you know how to harness it (see motivational speaker and author Dr Steinberg on how to harness stress and 'fall up' in Part 3).

Having to revise for, and take, an exam, for example, might be classified as short-term stress. In isolation, this would probably not cause any harm at all, it's only when stress accumulates and exceeds our coping ability without adequate recovery that it becomes a problem.

Imagine, for example, that you work for yourself and are a single parent. You are the only breadwinner, which you may cope admirably with, but then your mother gets ill and you can't afford to take time off to care for her. Situations like this, where there is one challenging situation on top of another, and seemingly no relief or way out, cause chronic stress and, if left unchecked, can lead to long-term mental problems like depression and anxiety – in short, completely destroying our reserves of inner strength.

HOW EXACTLY DOES STRESS DEPLETE OUR ABILITY TO BE RESILIENT?

Traumatic experiences are, by their very nature, stressful. And stress affects our ability to bounce back, so it's a double whammy! But what is it about stress itself that *does* that?

It's all about that fight or flight thing again: when we are stressed, our amygdala labels information coming in as threatening and it goes into over-drive, while our activity in the cerebral cortex – the part of the brain that allows us to make decisions, be sociable and take on new ideas – is severely restricted. As a result, you may act in ways you later regret. Ever flown off the handle at your child because you're stressed about something else? Or walked out of a restaurant because of an argument? Then you'll know what we mean by this. It's not only our mental health, however, that suffers – stress has a negative effect on our physical wellbeing too. (And as everyone knows, it's hard to feel mentally strong if we're physically under the weather.)

As we have already explored, when we are stressed, we release cortisol. Cortisol is an energizing hormone which increases blood sugar – great for the short term to react quickly, but in the long term it can be bad for our immune system. This is because a hormone called DHEA, which is released by the adrenal glands and which *supports* the immune system, cannot be released when cortisol is released. Furthermore, when blood sugar is raised it can lead to inflammation of artery walls – which is why stress is often a contributing factor to heart attacks and strokes.

One really important thing to remember when it comes to tackling stress is that if you give yourself adequate recovery time, you can not only take on more stress, but perform and thrive despite it.

GREGG STEINBERG ON THE IMPORTANCE OF RECOVERY TIME

'Our minds and bodies must have recovery time – especially where stress is concerned – that's why it's so important to take a holiday or break in the year. If you don't, you are headed for a tumble. Just look at how we build muscle. When we lift weights, we stress our muscles beyond normal levels. As an adaptive response to this overload, our muscles produce protein stimulating an increase in muscle fibre and muscle growth. However, if you continue to overload the muscles without giving them adequate recovery time, your muscles will shrink. Our muscles need recovery time to continue the growth cycle, and it's exactly the same with cognitive growth. When you take a holiday, you are giving yourself the needed recovery time to continue your growth cycle. In direct contrast, when you continue to work without taking a vacation or a short break, you will begin to shrink mentally and/or emotionally. This shrinkage may come in the form of loss of focus, increase in anxiety and depression and/or burnout.'

6. GETTING STUCK

In a way, all the strength robbers in this chapter are examples of getting psychologically 'stuck', or of unhelpful reactions you might have when something rattles your cage. That might be being overlooked for a promotion, having a row with your spouse, or learning your child is being bullied. The phrase 'these things are sent to test us' is a good one because it's so true: that is exactly what these setbacks in life do – they test our strength. It's how we react that counts.

Let's look at some of the common ways we get psychologically 'stuck' and how these can stop you thriving.

- **Stuck by your expectations:** Basically, the more fixated (stuck) you become on ideas of your life being a certain way, or on certain achievements, the more disappointed you will be if these don't happen. Disappointment is a very powerful emotion and can be very damaging in terms of our ability to bounce back. But disappointment itself comes from not managing your expectations, and so sometimes it's wise to take stock of these: what do I really want or expect from life? Am I frequently disappointed? Could it be that my expectations are too high?

- **Stuck with your goals:** Sometimes we can find ourselves putting lots of energy into a certain goal, only to stop and realize we've lost sight of why we're doing it in the first place. We often live on auto-pilot: pursuing goals because we think we should or because we think that's what society expects rather than because we want to, so it's really important to stop and evaluate your purpose occasionally, so that you don't waste energy doing things that your heart isn't in to.

- **Stuck with rigid thinking:** Rigid thinking feels logical in a way – it's thinking and doing things in the way that we always have, because we know what the outcome will be. However, we need to understand that just because we've dealt with something a certain way once, it doesn't mean this is the way we should deal with it now. Getting unstuck from rigid thinking is about developing a growth mindset and lateral thinking: what other options do I have for dealing with this issue? How can I approach it in a different way? We can radically change our thinking, but it takes time and effort and all too often we choose comfort over effort. By giving ourselves a calm space to think (using mindfulness techniques), and with a little discipline, we can loosen up our thinking, learn and grow.

- **Stuck by being too attached to outcomes:** We can't know what will happen when we begin a certain challenge, or when we do *anything* for that matter. Some people, however, become too attached to outcomes, and this normally leads to controlling behaviour. For example, if we give somebody a present, we can't control what their reaction will be; equally, we can't control what the outcome will be when we dare to enter into a relationship. Trying to control that outcome – demanding that the receiver of your gift gushes appropriately/demanding to know where you stand when three weeks into a relationship – are all just other ways we can get stuck in an unhelpful loop which prevents us from being open-minded and, therefore, more resilient.

- **Stuck comparing yourself to other people:** This is always a highway to nowhere because there will always be somebody better or worse off than you. Lurking on Facebook is especially dangerous because, by its very nature, people only put their 'best face' on there – their 'show highlights' if you like. So it may seem to you that everybody is going on fantastic holidays, getting married and generally having a much more exciting life than you – but that's because you don't see 'backstage' to their real lives. The problem is that we forget this, and very easily get sucked in, ending up feeling inadequate or even bitter and resentful – all of which are huge strength robbers.

❝ People get caught stuck in the loop of: 'I've set my goal and now I have to achieve it.' Sometimes it's helpful to stop and think: 'why am I striving for this?' ❞

Liggy Webb, consultant in behavioural skills and author of *Resilience*

ASK YOURSELF

Q What was your initial reason for pursuing the goal?

Q Is it still what you really want to do?

Q Are you clear on what this goal will bring you when you achieve it? What will it feel like? Will it give you what you want?

LIGGY WEBB ON THE IMPORTANCE OF LETTING GO

'I used to think that resilience was all about persistence and tenacity, but now I realize it's so much to do with knowing what to hold onto and what to let go of.

A really important part of being mentally strong is about having a light load in life. In other words, only taking on the things we really care about, being true to ourselves and our purpose. *But you have to spend time finding out what those are and you have to:*

- *Let go of things which aren't in line with your purpose.*
- *Let go of your ego. So many of us do things because we think we ought to, or because we want to impress other people. Let go of what other people think of you or what society expects.*
- *Let go of comparing yourself to other people – there will always be someone better off and worse off than you.'*

ASK YOURSELF

 What is happiness and success anyway? Is it about the volume of things you do or the quality? What project or commitment can you let go of today to make your load lighter and you feel more resilient?

7. AVOIDANCE AND OFFLOADING

> ❝ **Hurt doesn't go away simply because we don't acknowledge it. In fact, left unchecked, it festers, grows, and leads to behaviours that are completely out of line with who we want to be.** ❞

Brené Brown, research professor, University of Houston and author of *Rising Strong*

We saw in Part 1 how it is very natural to want to avoid pain. Trauma, change, adversity – they all put us under great stress and so it is perfectly normal to want to push that stress away. However, while this may work in the short term, in the long term avoidance just leads to greater stress levels because we are not processing our pain or trying to solve the situation – we are simply pushing it to one side. But it will rear its ugly head sooner or later.

One of the outcomes of attempting to ignore emotional pain is what author of *Rising Strong* Brené Brown calls 'chandeliering', where: 'We think we've packed the hurt so far down that it can't possibly resurface, yet all of a sudden a seemingly innocuous comment sends us into a rage or sparks a crying fit.' This is basically 'exploding' with the stress that we've tried to suppress.

Another very common way that we push away pain and fail to confront it is by offloading – literally pushing our pain onto other people. We're all guilty of it at some point: getting home from a terrible day at work and taking it out on our partner or loved ones; getting stressed with the kids because we're going through a hard time. The problem with this is that it makes us feel terrible about ourselves! And it sets us off on a spiral of self-loathing and regret which, in itself, eats away at our feelings of self-worth and resilience.

We hope you have learned a lot from this chapter. Chances are you recognize some strength robbers more than others but this, in itself, is a positive thing. Self-awareness, after all, is the first step in this journey of real strength, so make a note of those strength robbers you have a tendency to succumb to and, using the rest of this book to guide and support you, aim to work on these first.

REAL PEOPLE

"I learned I had to praise him for his efforts, not just his achievements." – *Kate*

Kate Prescott on how her son's perfectionism affected his ability to bounce back after failure (and how she helped him).

'My (now 13-year-old) son Charlie has always been very academic. Learning to read and write was a breeze for him – far easier than it was for his older brother – and consequently, right from being 4 or 5 years' old, people would always comment on his brains telling him, 'You're so clever/you're a genius!' My husband and I were guilty of it too and, I admit, I was proud when we were in a restaurant and, aged 4, he was able to read the menu. I made a fuss of him.

Once he started school, he got used to coming top in all the tests. Parent evening was a joy, all the teachers told us how conscientious he was and how easily he grasped things. Consequently, we'd get home and praise him for being 'so clever'. However, I began to notice that he wasn't as happy as his older brother, Freddie.

Freddie was less academic and more of a coaster at school. He had more friends and more interests. If he did badly in a test, he'd just say to himself 'best revise more next time'. Charlie, on the other hand, always got very stressed about tests (despite never doing badly in them), because it wasn't enough to do well: he had to come top.

One day, however, he came fourth in a French test (something that had never happened before) and he just fell apart. There were tears and tantrums: he was so angry with himself. I realized that day that his entire identity and self-worth came from being 'top of the class' so that when that didn't happen, he couldn't cope. He had so little experience of failure (as he saw it) that it floored him, whereas to Freddie – who experienced setbacks and failure much more often – it was like water off a duck's back. He just got back up.

Since that day, my husband and I have tried hard to praise Charlie for other things apart from getting 10 out of 10. We also try to praise his effort, rather than just his achievements, and encourage him to work at things that might not come so naturally, like sport, and then make a point of praising how hard he tried rather than how many goals he scored. Slowly, he's becoming more used to not being perfect at things, and more open to 'having a go' whatever the outcome. I see a much more resilient child now – and probably a happier one.'

3 HOW CAN YOU BUILD REAL STRENGTH?

CHAPTER 7

MANAGE YOUR EMOTIONS

hen we come across a challenge in life, or go through a bad patch, it's usually not the events themselves that cause the most trouble – it's our emotions. When it comes to pursuing and trying to build resilience, emotions are like our Achilles heel. Let's face it, if it weren't for those pesky feelings getting in the way, colouring our decisions and provoking reactions, things would be a hell of a lot easier! If you've ever stormed out of a difficult meeting because you're filled with rage, or sent an email you regret because you're so consumed with jealousy, you'll know what we mean. In short: you can have all the determination and good intentions in the world, but when strong emotions take over, it can feel so very hard to stay strong.

The good news is there is plenty you can do to learn to regulate and manage your emotions better so that they work *for*, not against, you, meaning you feel in control and, ultimately, stronger.

KNOW YOURSELF

> **❝In terms of building the best possible platform to bounce back to, it really is important first of all, to know and understand who you really are.❞**
>
> Liggy Webb, consultant in behavioural skills and author of *Resilience*

In Part 1, we touched upon self-awareness and how it was the first step in the journey towards real strength. Managing your emotions is a vital part of building real strength, and so it would follow that self-awareness is the first step in that journey too. Think about it: how can you begin to tackle and regulate your emotions without first of all becoming aware of them? This means recognizing them and getting curious about them; watching how they shift and change and, crucially, how they affect your behaviour and ability to tackle whatever struggle you come up against.

66Resilience is more available to people curious about their own line of thinking and behaving.99

Brené Brown, research professor, University of Houston and author of *Rising Strong*

In Brené Brown's book *Rising Strong,* she talks about being 'triggered'. This is the first stage of the rising-after-adversity process, which she has coined as the 'Rising Strong' process. Being triggered refers to that moment where something happens which sets your emotions off. You know that moment where you feel emotionally wobbly? This might be due to something relatively minor, such as an argument with a colleague, or finding out you've been overlooked for a promotion, or something more serious, like finding out your partner has been unfaithful.

In *Rising Strong*, Brown likens our struggles to being 'in an arena' and our 'trigger' as that 'face down moment'. In other words, that moment when you have been knocked to the floor. A trigger is anything that creates emotional conflict and it's when we're in emotional conflict that our feelings can get the better of us. The result of this might be that we tell ourselves unhelpful narratives about ourselves and other people: *They're all getting at me, I can't do this, it's my fault* etc. Or that we begin to engage in behaviours or coping strategies which only rob us of our strength. The 'Rising Strong' process that Brown sets out is an alternative to this.

The question that you're probably asking now though is: if the first stage of that process is being face down in the arena, how do I get back up? Well it's here that 'know yourself' comes into its own, since the most important thing is to recognize you have been knocked down – 'triggered' – in the first place. Once you know you've been emotionally triggered, you can begin to look at those emotions, and possibly see patterns: *Oh, so I tend to feel angry when someone accuses me of not doing my best*, or, *I feel a lot of guilt around parenting.*

We can then hold those emotions under our metaphorical microscope and get curious about them, learn from them: what are these emotions really about and where do they come from? How are they stopping me from being strong? And, perhaps more importantly, how can I better use them to *help* me be strong?

BRENÉ BROWN ON HOW TO KNOW WHEN YOU'VE BEEN EMOTIONALLY TRIGGERED[1]

'To realize you've been triggered, you need to get 'curious' about where you've been to get to this point. Only then can you envisage a course of action for the future. It's helpful to dig backwards into the process and ask yourself certain key questions:

1. *Where have I come from to feel like this?*
2. *Where did it start?*
3. *How are my thoughts and emotions affecting my behaviours?*

Staying connected to your body is also very important: What sets your heart off racing, or that tense feeling in your chest? Train yourself to see patterns in your behaviour in order that the alarm bell sounds when you're triggered. For

---

[1] Sourced from a phone interview with Brené Brown by Katy Regan in 2015.

me, when I either want to punch somebody, eat carbs, or start plotting a revenge narrative, I know it's more likely I am vulnerable and afraid – not really angry.

The problem is, a lot of us were not raised to get curious about emotions – and it creates unnecessary conflict. If someone 'triggers' you by sending what you feel is a curt email, rather than stew over what you think their story is, ask them. Say, 'Hey, I just wanted to check everything is ok between us because I didn't know if you were frustrated or just firing off your emails …' Chances are they may say, 'I'm so glad you asked, because I am pissed off but not with you.' So be curious, not just about yourself and your triggers, but other people's too.'

MAKE A NOTE WHEN YOU HAVE BEEN 'TRIGGERED'

When you feel you have been 'triggered', write it on a Post It note, type it into your phone, or send yourself an email with what happened. Make a point of looking back over these once a month. Over time, you will amass enough notes on your own unhelpful behaviours for you to spot any destructive or avoidant patterns. You can then come up with a course of action to stop that happening in the future.

HARNESSING YOUR EMOTIONAL AGILITY

We are all emotional beings – admittedly, some more than others! Either way, we can't stop emotions happening. Like birds on a feeding table, they're constantly flying in, some staying (longer if we feed them) and some flying off again almost as soon as they arrived. The question is: how do you experience emotions – especially the tricky ones – in a way that does not compromise your ability to be strong, and enables you to uphold your values?

This is where 'emotional agility' comes in. Just like resilience, stamina, perseverance and real strength, there are a gazillion interpretations of emotional agility. If we break it right down, however, to those two words, it is basically the ability to be agile with our emotions. That is, to be able to understand, harness them and use them to the best of our ability, in order to be more in control of them (not them of us!). In a nutshell, emotional agility enables us to take control of our feelings.

Getting hooked

In her book, *Emotional Agility*, and the TED talk of the same name, psychologist and author Susan David describes that moment when your emotion(s) is triggered as getting 'hooked'.

> **"When we are hooked we only see one perspective, one line of thought."**
>
> Susan David, psychologist and author of *Emotional Agility*

It's important to remember that it doesn't just have to be reacting strongly in an overt way to an emotion that proves that we're hooked. Brooding (ruminating) is another way of showing we're hooked, as well as bottling up emotions and suppressing them. In all of these hooked states, there is no space between the stimulus to what we're feeling and the way we're dealing with it. We have – in other words – pushed ourselves into an emotional corner and left ourselves no choice, no other available decisions and no alternative behaviours. When we're hooked like this, we're rigid in our thinking – the opposite of emotional agility. However, if we can learn to create a gap between feeling the emotion and reacting to it, we can tackle adversity much better, even overcome it. The ability to do this is at the very core of emotional agility.

BE THE NUTRITIONIST FOR YOUR SOUL

Imagine you are hosting a dinner party for your emotions. It's up to you which ones you feed. Would you put more focus on those emotions that are already draining you, or do you want to give more energy towards those emotions that make you feel happy?

Getting *unhooked*

At its core, real strength is how we deal with the everyday challenges that life throws at us and deal with the situations and thoughts that we have. Learning how to 'unhook' from negative thoughts and emotions is an extremely useful and important skill. Sometimes, it is actual emotions that we are hooked by, but sometimes it's the ideas about how we want our lives to be (even – and especially – if they're not like that). An example of this might be not being able to afford to move house and then hearing of a friend, who seems to have it very easy, buying the house of their dreams! If we're not careful, envy and bitterness can eat us up, even if, when we think about it, their house purchase bears no relation to our life. Emotions then start to dominate our actions, rather than our values, and we can slide very easily from fact to opinion to judgement. So 'my friend has bought a house she loves and our time will come' turns to, 'it's not fair! How come they can afford just to buy a house and we have to struggle (cue more brooding). What wrong choices have I made in life/what have I done to deserve this?'

If we can become aware of and open up that space between the fact and the judgement, however, we can become 'unhooked' and more emotionally agile.

How to become unhooked

1. Show up

By this we mean recognize your thoughts and emotions for what they are – thoughts and emotions. If you are in a meeting and you notice you are being undermined, it's about having the thought: 'I'm being undermined – I'm having the thought that I'm being undermined. I'm having the emotion that I'm being undermined.' This is opposed to the alternative thought of, 'How dare they undermine me, I'm going to storm out!'

Stop fighting against them, or 'drop the rope' as Susan David says. 'Don't treat emotions as facts, but understand they can be guides' she says in the talk. 'See that gnaw you have in your chest? That's a beacon – a guide to what's important to you, but it's still not a fact.' For example, feeling guilty that you don't spend enough time with your kids does not mean you *don't* spend enough time with your kids. However, that feeling is a good indicator of what you want and what matters to you right now – you want to spend more time with your kids.

2. Create the space (between stimulus and response)

In Chapter 9 we will be looking in a little more depth at ways in which you can separate yourself from your thoughts and emotions, so that you can look at them objectively. But for now, all you need to know is that creating a 'metaview' is a psychological term for being able to rise above your thoughts and feelings, like a helicopter. It means being able to step above the emotion and realize that a purely emotional, rather than cognitive, response is not helpful. It's realizing you need to respond in line with your values. The ability to do this is vital to our wellbeing. It's why, explains David, when a child comes home from school and says they're being bullied, it's important not to simply try and take their pain away from them by treating them to ice-cream or playing with them. Instead, ask a child what's important to them – how they want to 'be' in this difficult situation. This will help them to do what they want to do, even if their peers say and do something else. This of course goes for grown-ups too! The habits that we create which are imbued with our values make the most difference to our lives and our happiness. So next time you have a thought or emotion and are reacting to it, ask yourself the following questions.

ASK YOURSELF

Ⓠ Is this choice in how I am reacting bringing me closer to the person I want to be?

Ⓠ Could I choose an alternative behaviour that would bring me closer?

3. Step out/let go

Not all 'hooks' are bad ones, but there are some that we really need to let go of (for example, the narrative 'I'll always be the fat one' or 'I'm no good at dating'). These hooks are keeping us 'unagile' and so 'stepping out' is just another way of letting go of them. An important part of the 'letting go' part of emotional agility is (and we've touched on this before) knowing which hooks to let go of, and which to hold onto. The response to that is very simple: those that are imbued with our values we should hold onto, because we are much more mentally strong if we cultivate deep values and do things that are in line with them. It makes being emotionally agile a whole lot easier.

4. Make changes and move forward

This stage is all about making tiny changes. It's the small changes, after all, the tiny shifts in our habits, which make an overall difference to our life. The important thing to remember if we want to remain strong and also to build strength, is that those changes need to be deeply linked to our 'want to' goals and our values.

CONDITION YOUR THINKING

At the core of our brainstem, we have a bundle of nerve cells called the 'reticular activating system' or RAS for short. The RAS contains 70% of the brain's nerve cells, and has a few extremely important functions:

- It is the portal through which nearly all information enters the brain.
- It takes instructions and information from your conscious mind and passes them to your subconscious.
- It acts as the 'gatekeeper' to filter or screen the type of information that will be allowed to get through.
- Think of it also like the key to switching on your awareness. As such, we can programme it to pay attention or 'switch on' to whatever emotion or goal we choose, helping us to achieve positive outcomes.

In his book, *Getting Things Done*, productivity consultant Dave Allen explains the function and potential of the reticular activating system further:

> *'Just like a computer, your brain has a search function – but it's even more phenomenal than a computer's as it seems to be programmed by what we focus on, and more primarily, what we identify with.'*

By 'what we identify with', Allen means the specific things that we, as individuals, hone in on due to our past experiences, our jobs, our cultural references – and all the things that make us who we are. For example, an optician will notice people wearing glasses more than your average person; a pregnant woman will suddenly notice other pregnant women.

TRAIN YOUR MIND

Think about the colour red. Then look around your environment. You will immediately notice whatever red there is, even if it's the tiniest bit. Similarly, you can train your RAS to notice certain things.

Refocusing your attention on what's important

Taking Allen's description of the RAS as our brain's 'search function', we can understand that if we can programme it to 'search' for and pay attention to the things we want to achieve, then it can help us to achieve them. Basically, the RAS has the power to bring to your attention all the necessary information to help you achieve your goal. It can identify resources that would otherwise have gone unnoticed and drive your attention towards positive outcomes.

The RAS also has a part to play in managing our emotions. This is because we feed it with thoughts and internal self-talk all the time. And so it follows that if we make these thoughts and self-talk positive, our RAS will latch onto those and use them to achieve positive outcomes.

"With the power of positive attention we can programme our minds to produce new outcomes."

Liggy Webb, consultant in behavioural skills and author of *Resilience*

One great way of making the most of your RAS and building your inner strength and confidence is to visualize outcomes that you want to achieve. Visualization is basically the act of creating vivid and compelling images in your mind which emulate, as closely as possible, the real thing. The interesting thing about your RAS is that it can't tell the difference between visualizing a task and actually doing it – it uses the same processes. In other words it tends to believe whatever message you give it. Therefore, if you were to practise/visualize feeling supremely confident as you give a speech, this would improve your ability to confidently give the actual speech.

FEED YOUR MIND WITH POSITIVE THOUGHTS AND EMOTIONS

Remember YOU control your RAS, it doesn't control you, so pay attention to what and how you are feeding it. The more you feed it with positive thoughts and emotions, the more chance you will have to develop that all-important positive attitude and cultivate optimism. For example, when faced with a tough work challenge or deadline, instead of thinking 'this is going to be hard and I'm going to hate it', redirect yourself to think 'I'm going to find a way to enjoy this, no matter what'.

In this chapter, we have explored the part our emotions play in our behaviours, the decisions we make and our ability to be strong. Hopefully, you have learned strategies and tips to help you to first of all recognize the emotions you are feeling and then regulate and manage them better. One of the main points was creating that all-important space between the trigger for our emotion and how we react to it. We talked about creating a 'metaview', which is one great way to do this, but in Chapter 9 we will be discussing further how we can create a space between ourselves and our thoughts. It's worth noting that these techniques can be used to create a space from our emotions, too, so take extra notice when you come to that part. And above all, remember, you control your emotions – they don't control you!

ASK YOURSELF

Q   What bad 'hooks' do I have in my life? For example, the story I tell myself about how I'm no good at relationships, or how I'll never move up in my career

Q   What 'good' hooks do I have? In other words, ones that are imbued with my deepest values. For example, I really want to volunteer for a charity or I want to be a more 'present' parent. (Hint: keep hold of those good hooks!)

Q   What steps can I take to feed my RAS with more positive, helpful thoughts? Is there a way I can stop myself when I'm feeding it with negative ones?

CHAPTER 8

THE TWO Cs: COMPASSION AND CONNECTEDNESS

> **"If we can cultivate courage, compassion and connection we can feel 'good' and 'enough' and 'worthy' – we can live a wholehearted life."**
>
> Brené Brown, research professor, University of Houston and author of *Rising Strong*

THE POWER OF COMPASSION

We've already talked about the importance of vulnerability when it comes to building real strength. In fact, your willingness to show and embrace your vulnerability – your fallibility, your shame and your fears – is not just important, but vital to growth and resilience against all life throws at you. But there is another factor we haven't talked about yet that is also a vital contributor to what we might call 'The Andrex Effect' – the importance of being soft *and* strong: compassion.

> **"Both self-compassion and compassion towards other people is a major part of maintaining and building strength."**
>
> Dr Michael Sinclair, Consultant Psychologist

Before we explore why that is, and how you can develop compassion in order to strengthen you from the inside out, let's define it.

What *is* compassion?

The *Oxford Dictionary* definition of compassion is: 'sympathetic pity and concern for the sufferings or misfortunes of others'.

Chances are, when you hear the word 'compassion' you think of kindness. But while kindness (not to mention sympathy and concern) play a part, actually scientific study has found that the core of compassion is courage.

You might be thinking: is there really a scientific study of compassion? The answer is yes! Paul Gilbert, Professor of Clinical Psychology at the University of Derby, has been researching shame and shame-based difficulties for the last 35 years, and he developed Compassion Focused Therapy to treat it. Compassion Focused Therapy is a type of psychotherapy and its foundation is 'compassion mind training' — in other words, learning how to be more compassionate towards yourself and other people. Gilbert also launched the Compassionate Mind Foundation, and on the foundation's website he defines compassion as:

> 'A sensitivity to suffering in self and others with a commitment to try to alleviate and prevent it.'

The 'courage' part, Gilbert explains, lies in the willingness (that word again) to explore the nature and the causes of suffering:

> 'The challenge is to acquire the wisdom we need to address the causes of suffering in ourselves, and others.'

Why do we need to learn self-compassion?

Imagine you've just come back home after an interview that didn't go well. You might beat yourself up: 'I'm useless, why didn't I prepare more?' It wouldn't take you long, however, to realize that if you engage with that self-criticism it very quickly affects your confidence and ability to feel resilient. You may not, for example, want to go to any more interviews.

A more compassionate approach, on the other hand, can keep resilience alive. Consultant Counselling Psychologist Dr Michael Sinclair explains: 'If we imagine sex or food, we have a whole physical arousal around it – we have an emotional and physical reaction: our mouth waters, the pulse quickens. If we bring a more compassionate self-talk to our experiences [say, of the interview after-math], the same happens: we have an emotional and physical reaction: we feel immediately calmer, safer and soothed.'

And therefore, it would follow, emotionally stronger.

But how does it work?

Well, it's partly to do with the power of the mind: basically, what and how we think affects our wellbeing. When you are self-critical, you have a bully in your head. Self-criticizing makes you feel more anxious and more vulnerable; it even changes your physical posture. Whereas, if you practise self-kindness, you will naturally feel soothed: thoughts lead to feelings.

There is also a biological explanation: instead of releasing cortisol (the stress hormone), when we're in the compassionate 'state' or gear we release oxytocin, which is the same hormone that lactating/nursing mothers produce. Just as it makes the baby feel soothed and safe, it does the same thing to us. The release of oxytocin gives us that sense of wellbeing and strength. We start to believe, 'it'll be ok, I'm safe, I can cope with this'.

What is Compassion Focused Therapy?

So back to the therapy that Professor Gilbert developed – the elements of which you can easily practise yourself to cultivate more self-kindness.

As we've already touched upon, Compassion Focused Therapy (CFT) is a type of psychotherapy particularly useful for those suffering from deep feelings of shame and guilt – things we all suffer from, from time to time, but which rob us of our inner strength.

Biological evolution forms the backbone of CFT, that is, this idea that the way we think, and the way our brains are wired, is down to evolution.

Professor Gilbert believes that we have three regulation systems, or three modes of thinking and reacting:

- **The Threat System:** this relates to fear and anxiety, that primeval way of protecting ourselves we've already talked about, when sensing threat to our physical and emotional wellbeing.

- **The Drive System:** this involves emotions and thoughts (and chemicals) that make us determined and motivated to achieve goals. This system can make us feel quite single-minded and determined about things, often in adverse situations. It's that 'I won't let this get the better of me!' feeling.

- **The Shooting System:** this helps us feel safe. It activates in stressful situations when the other systems aren't working. But it's a very natural, evolutionary state and this is where the compassionate mind and the basis of compassionate training come in. When we're in an adverse and stressful state, we can use this system to calm down, feel safer and think rationally.

When we're self-critical, our thoughts become threat-focused: what if the interviewer thought I was an idiot? What if I can't ever go to an interview again? This is our Threat System in action – in other words, our flight or fight system – and we act irrationally, trying to run away from or eradicate the threat. The problem is, though, when we're in that state, we can't reflect. We're just running away and that affects our resilience and ability to grow and learn from our experience – to thrive going forward.

When we are in the compassionate mind (the Soothing System), we are in a safer, calmer space and are more able to rationalize and think coolly about how to move on and help ourselves in a wise way.

The central technique of Compassion Focused Therapy is Compassionate Mind Training (CMT), which teaches skills and attributes of compassion. CMT helps transform problematic patterns of thinking and emotions related to anxiety, shame, self-criticism and depersonalization (separating yourself from your pain) into more helpful patterns of thinking that enable us to calm down and think rationally.

DR MICHAEL SINCLAIR ON GETTING INTO THE COMPASSIONATE MIND

- *'First of all, we need to bring mindful awareness to our experience, rather than ignoring our suffering or exacerbating it. So start off by simply noticing and being aware of your thoughts and feelings when you are feeling distressed.*

- *Recognize the common humanity – i.e. the fact that, even though the specific circumstances of a situation might be different, we all suffer with painful emotions and troublesome thoughts, and we're all in the same boat. Actually say out loud to yourself (or silently if you wish): "I'm feeling sad. This is a moment/a day of sadness. Other people suffer like this, we all struggle in life; I am not alone in my suffering."*

- *Practise self-kindness – rather than being judgemental and critical towards yourself, be understanding and talk to yourself as you'd talk to a friend – what advice would you give them? What words of support would you offer? Perhaps, simply acknowledging that "This is really difficult".'*

IMAGINE THE ADVICE OF YOUR WISEST FRIEND

Close your eyes and think of someone you consider to be really wise. Now imagine what they would say to you in this situation – what advice would they give you?

Be kind to yourself

In her book *Rising Strong*, researcher and author Brené Brown takes us through the 'Rising Strong' process she identified and developed for what she calls 'getting up after a fall' or, in other words, overcoming whatever adversity comes our way.

Compassion is a big part of this process and is something that can be learnt by anyone.

In fact, in order to help understand how to cultivate and practise self-compassion, let's look at the 'rising strong' process.

Brown breaks it down into three specific parts: the Reckoning, the Rumble and the Revolution. It's a multi-faceted process (not to mention a fascinating one) that can be described as follows:

1. **The Reckoning:** This is the part when you realize you have been 'triggered'. This simply means realizing something has happened that has knocked you emotionally off course. In other words, it's coming into contact with adversity.
2. **The Rumble:** This is the stage where you explore your feelings and emotions around the situation you find yourself in. What stories are you telling yourself about your predicament? Are they true or untrue? If you dig beneath the surface of what's

happened – what emotions are you really rumbling with here?
Jealousy, fear or self-righteousness, for example.

3. **The Revolution:** This is when you use what you've learned in
the Rumble part to grow and change as a person.

If we are wise, it's in the Rumble part of this process that we
can take the opportunity to cultivate self-compassion. As we've
already discussed, self-awareness is always the first step in any
journey of personal growth and it's the same when trying to grow
compassion. So, the first thing to do is to get curious about our
thoughts and feelings.

Brown outlines three vital questions in her book that we should
ask ourselves while rumbling with a difficult situation or trauma.
Doing this can really help us to develop compassion and therefore
build inner strength.

1. **What more do I need to learn and understand about the
difficult situation I find myself in?**

   For example, say you have fallen out with your mother
   and it's causing you great distress, what more could you
   understand about the conflict? How did the argument start?
   Who – if anyone – started it? What other factors were affecting
   things – for example, were you both tired? Had you been
   drinking? Could this row actually be about something else
   entirely? Something deeper, that with more reflection (and
   compassion!) you could excavate?

2. **What more do I need to learn and understand about the people
in the story?**

   What was your mother's standpoint in the row? Were other
   people discussed or involved in the argument? What were
   their parts in it? Get curious and examine the details
   because the more you understand, the more you will build
   your capacity for compassion.

3. **What more do I need to learn and understand about myself?**

   Look closely at your reactions: are you engaging in familiar behavioural patterns? Are these helpful or working for you? And if not, why not? Could you come at the problem or situation from a different perspective?

The importance of boundaries when it comes to compassion

We've already established that developing and exercising compassion, both in terms of ourselves and other people, not only makes us feel stronger, but helps to build more strength too. It's quite basic really: when we are nice to ourselves and other people, we feel better. And when we feel better and happier, we feel stronger.

One thing that might surprise you, however, is that being compassionate does not mean always putting yourself out, saying 'yes' to everything and generally being a martyred saint. In fact, on the contrary, all those things are likely to drain your inner reserves of strength. Interestingly, through her research, Brené Brown, author of *Rising Strong*, discovered that rather than the people who put themselves out all the time, it was the ones who had the most defined and well-respected boundaries who were the most compassionate. Why is this? 'Because their boundaries keep them out of resentment', she says.

It makes perfect sense if we do not place value on our own time and what we can and cannot do – or more importantly, what we want and do not want to do – then we cannot expect other people to. What happens then is that we become resentful and bitter and end up feeling taken for granted – all of which are emotions and experiences that drain us of our strength and resources. If we can learn to enforce healthy boundaries, then we can avoid this.

What's more, we will be living with more honesty and integrity – a life that is in line with our values.

BRENÉ BROWN ON BOUNDARIES AND HOW TO ENFORCE HEALTHY ONES[1]

'Boundaries are no more than clarity about what is and isn't ok. Setting them requires sharing that with someone and then holding them accountable to what you set forth. The problem is, we tend to keep our boundaries internal and then when someone violates them, we're angry – and the person doesn't even know what they did. Or, we make explicit what's ok and what's not, then when someone violates that, we don't hold them accountable because it's uncomfortable, which basically says those boundaries were not that important to me in the first place.'

[1]Sourced from a phone interview with Brené Brown by Katy Regan in 2015.

Another way in which to cultivate our capacity for compassion is to be courageous enough to wade into our darkness. By this, we mean to confront our worst fears and our weaknesses, to acknowledge our failures and embrace our pain. After all, it is only when we know our own dark side that we can be truly compassionate to others going through their darkness – that we can begin to know how they feel.

66 Appreciating and valuing yourself is the most important component of self-love. 99

Liggy Webb, consultant in behavioural skills and author of *Resilience*

Perhaps it's worth remembering too that a great by-product of developing and practising compassion is that we stop comparing ourselves to other people and judge others less. Instead, when we practise compassion, we look for and see what is good in ourselves and others and, in turn, show the very best side of ourselves. Since comparing oneself and the envy and feelings of injustice that can bring are all huge strength robbers, this is a major bonus!

THE POWER OF CONNECTION

There is a lot to be said for the old adage 'no man is an island'. We all need to be and to feel connected to be at our strongest; we all need the support of other people to get through tough times.

In her TED talk, 'The Power of Vulnerability', researcher Brené Brown explores connection – our need for it – and its relation to courage and vulnerability. Wanting to explore her own feelings of shame and 'not being good enough', Brené set out on a massive research project which became her TED talk and book of the same name. The research basically involved interviewing thousands of people about their stories of shame, vulnerability and connection, and what she found was this:

- We, as human beings, need to connect and to belong. It's what sets us apart from other mammals and it's what gives our lives purpose and meaning.

- We understand deep down that in order for this connection that we crave to happen, we need to be really 'seen'. This means, we have to be able to reveal our WHOLE self, warts and all.

- The problem is that we feel very vulnerable doing this, because we fear that when people see our whole self, there may be something about us which makes us unworthy of that connection.

- So this vulnerability or shame is really our fear of not connecting: what if I'm not good enough? What if, when people see the real me, I won't be worthy of connection?
- In her thousands of interviews, however, Brown discovered that what separated those who had a strong sense of belonging and connection and those who struggle, was that the former group believed they were *worthy* of belonging and connection.

So how can this help build up resilience and inner strength?

- Perhaps the most important thing is that feeling connected and like we belong is at the root of real strength.
- Put another way, the biggest thing stopping us feeling strong is feeling disconnected.
- We can improve our ability to connect, and therefore to be emotionally stronger, if we are courageous enough to be vulnerable – to show our whole selves.

Set out in this way, we can see how connection, belonging, vulnerability, courage and strength are all interconnected.

Loneliness makes us less resilient

We are becoming a more isolated society and this is affecting our ability to tackle and manage crises and to bounce back – as well as our physical health. This is why:

> 66 **In times of adversity … it becomes increasingly important to make positive connections with those around you.** 99

Liggy Webb, consultant in behavioural skills and author of *Resilience*

If our expectations of social contact are not met, our body alerts us that something is wrong. We feel physically threatened. If the loneliness persists it starts to interfere with our ability to regulate the emotions that we associate with loneliness. This basically means that things get blown out of proportion: our sadness, fears for the future, fears there's something inherently 'wrong with us' increase and distort the way we see ourselves in relation to others.

Tests by US psychologists Roy Baumeister and Jean Twenge showed that the *expectation* of isolation reduces our willpower and perseverance. This is manifested by our struggle to control our habits and behaviour. For example, we might engage in more destructive behaviours like smoking, drinking and casual sex for instant gratification, but these only increase our sense of aloneness and reduce our resilience. Lonely people report more exposure to stress and are more likely to withdraw from engaging with others, which makes them even more lonely. More interestingly, perhaps, loneliness and lack of connection with other people actually affects our cardiovascular system and our immune system.

On the flipside, relationships are good for us! Love promotes health and strengthens the immune system and our cardiovascular functions. In 2007, the 'Focus on Family' report by the Office for National Statistics reported that married people of both sexes had better health. It's not just about spouses or partners though. People with a good circle of close friends reap health benefits. In 2006, a study of 3000 nurses with breast cancer found that women without close friends were four times more likely to die than those with 10 or more friends.

How can we become more connected?

So, if the secret to resilience is connection, the question that poses itself is: how can we become more connected? By working on our relationships – that's it in a nutshell, isn't it? Relationships with other people are our main source of connection. They are also our main source of support when going through tough times. But there is also growing evidence to say that our relationships with other people influence hugely how we cope in the face of crisis. In other words, how resilient we are.

The more support you can draw from the people around you, the more confidence you will have in your ability to get through what you need to get through. And it's not the number of friends or people in your life that matter, either, it's the quality of those relationships, so being able to create and then tend to them is a hugely important life skill for real strength. In order to maintain healthy relationships, it is vital to know:

- How they work and what is expected of you as a partner in a relationship.
- Not to take them for granted.
- To make commitments and put in the time necessary to keep them in good shape.

Let's explore ways to do all of the above:

- **Talking:** by sharing our thoughts, feelings and struggles, we increase our own and other peoples' understanding of them and therefore our feelings of connection.
- **Appreciate family:** our family members are the people we are most likely to neglect or take for granted, but they also offer the most potential for deep, meaningful connections. So try to appreciate and accept who your mother, father, sister is, rather than trying to change them; work with what you have, rather than bemoaning what you don't.
- **Random acts of kindness:** being kind causes elevated levels of dopamine in the brain and so we get a natural high,

often referred to as 'Helper's High'. Acts of kindness are often accompanied by emotional warmth. Emotional warmth produces the hormone, oxytocin, in the brain and throughout the body – it's the same 'soothing' hormone we learned about in the 'compassion' section. Acts of kindness can range from volunteering to simply giving someone a compliment. Telling someone they look nice or have lost weight can give them – and you – a glow that lasts the day.

Connect to your purpose and find meaning in your life

'Connection' does not have to mean connecting with other people, it can be about connecting to your PURPOSE. Having a purpose means having a reason to do something and it leads to other wonderful things in relation to real strength. If we have a purpose in life we are more likely to be:

* Determined and driven.
* Happier.
* Have higher self esteem.
* Therefore, more resilient.

A great deal of research suggests that people who have purpose and meaning in their life are healthier, more resilient, happier, and more in control of their lives. They also experience less stress, anxiety and bouts of depression.

We need purpose in life just as we need to feel like we belong and connect to others, because we need to feel like we are adding value. Knowing our purpose guides us in how we choose to live our lives and what we choose to strive for over other things. In short, having purpose connects us to ourselves.

REAL PEOPLE

"Being diagnosed with a tumour helped me for the better." *- Liggy*

Liggy Webb on how she developed self-compassion following a personal trauma.

'In January 2015 I went to New Zealand for my parents' 60th wedding anniversary. I felt exhausted when I got back. My parents were in their 80s and had more energy than me – so I knew something wasn't quite right. I kept waking up, with the feeling that my heart was dropping. I was tired, a bit short of breath but, above all, I just didn't feel right.

I was sent for an echocardiogram and they said that, actually, I had a really healthy heart but they found a benign tumour which was blocking my heart valve. They had to remove it because if they didn't, it would be fatal. It was a big daunting operation and I knew that in order to get to the point of recovery, I had to reach the point of acceptance.

The operation took place in May 2016. The recovery part is hard. They have to cut through a lot of muscle and bone and all your ribs are broken, but I discovered, two really important things which helped me: I was observing my response to the situation and I was curious. I thought about all the things I had learnt about resilience and how to put it into action now that I was faced with the biggest challenge I had ever experienced.

I've always looked at life in terms of 'probortunities' – i.e. I've always looked at problematic situations and thought 'what is the opportunity in this?' I have also learnt a great deal about self-compassion and self-care – I realized that in order to get through this, I had to let go of my inner control freak and learn to trust being in the hands and care of others.

When you go into hospital, it can be very easy to go into victim mode; to put your pyjamas on and adopt a 'fix me' mentality. I learnt how important it is to work in partnership with the care team in the hospital to really aid positive recovery.

My heart surgeon Alan Bryan and the staff at the Bristol Heart Institute and I have since gone back to work with them, delivering resilience workshops as a way of saying thank you for everything that they have done for me. I was in hospital for just over a week and I became very good friends with someone called Laura who was on the same ward as me. We really bonded and talked about other things we loved and were grateful for to keep our minds off what we were physically going through.

Being diagnosed with the tumour, in a strange way, was one of the best things that has happened to me. I believe that I've changed for the better because of it. Certainly I've slowed down and I'm much calmer and kinder to myself than I used to be. I don't feel disappointed anymore if I can't do or have something, I'm just grateful I can do anything at all.

I also used to be very attached to the outcome of things and I'm much better at living with uncertainty. Embracing the concept of mindfulness has helped me to live more in the moment. I used to be very ambitious about what I was able to achieve in a day and always piling up my to-do list. Now I fully recognize the importance of balancing my life and my personal energy and appreciating and respecting each precious moment. It was also great to know that I truly walk my talk as far as resilience is concerned!'

ASK YOURSELF

Ⓠ Think of a current difficult situation you're experiencing. Now, imagine what advice you would give to a friend in the same situation. Write this advice down, or record yourself saying it.

Ⓠ For this same situation, write a list of all your thoughts and feelings around it. Now do the same for the other people involved in it – what might they be thinking/ feeling? What story might they be telling themselves about the situation?

Ⓠ Do you sometimes over-commit? Say 'yes' when you really mean 'no' and don't want to do something? How could you practise saying 'no' in a more compassionate way?

CHAPTER 9

BUILDING ON YOUR RESILIENCE EVERY DAY

A s we approach the end of the book, we hope that by now you are feeling more confident about your ability to overcome whatever you are going through. Like all skills, however, building resilience and real strength is not something you do overnight, nor is it something that you learn once and that's it for life. Instead, think of real strength as a psychological muscle: you have to work at it to make it strong in the first place, then you have to *keep* working at it to *keep* it strong. 'Use it, or lose it' goes for resilience like it goes for learning languages, maintaining a good memory and all other cognitive skills. This final chapter, then, is full of real skills and techniques that you can take away and try right now; techniques that you can turn to when you feel you've hit a tricky patch. All you have to do is to digest and understand what each step of each process entails, and then you can turn to them whenever you need them, ensuring that your real strength muscle remains in the best shape it can.

ENCOURAGE MORE HELPFUL WAYS OF THINKING

Just as we can't stop bad things happening to us, we also can't stop how these things make us feel – anxious, stressed or even depressed.

Cognitive Behavioural Therapy (CBT) is a type of psychotherapy which has been used to treat depression and stress for years. In very basic terms, it helps the client to control and reduce their symptoms (of stress, anxiety, depression) by giving them coping strategies and helping them to change the way they think about their situation, which, in turn, changes their emotions and behaviour.

Acceptance and Commitment Therapy (ACT) is also a form of psychotherapy but is a step on from the 'new CBT' if you like.

While CBT is more about controlling your symptoms of distress when you come up against a setback or trauma in your life, ACT is more concerned with the *relationship* you have with your symptoms. Using mindfulness and also 'acceptance' techniques, ACT invites people not to avoid or eliminate unpleasant feelings, but to sit with them and get curious about them, in order to move towards what therapists and psychologists call a more 'value-based life'. In other words, ACT encourages us towards more helpful ways of thinking which means we don't just feel more able to tackle the challenges we have, but to live the life we are meant to live while we do that.

> 66 **If we can learn to experience stress and respond to it in a more helpful way then we can feel less distressed and stronger.** 99
>
> Dr Michael Sinclair, Consultant Psychologist

We already know from Part 1 that when we experience some adversity, our normal response is to try to control or eradicate it in some way. However, we also know that when we do this, we exacerbate those feelings and the situation becomes all-consuming. We become obsessed and pre-occupied with our problem, leaving less time and energy for the things that are important to us.

The question ACT asks is: is this workable for you? Is this making you feel good and enabling to live the life you want? Because if it is, that's great, but if it's not then you need to look at your relationship to the thoughts and feelings you're having. The first thing to do might be to stop fighting altogether, so that you can really explore what you're feeling.

66 If we stay still, we give ourselves opportunities to see alternative routes out. You don't have to struggle. Do nothing. 99

Dr Michael Sinclair, Consultant Psychologist

So how can I encourage more helpful ways of thinking?

ACT is a technique that can do just that. It is something that is practised by professional psychotherapists, but if you understand each of the four stages, there is no reason why you can't take the concepts from each and practise it yourself.

1. **Wake up!**

   This step is all about being present in the here and now. One way of cultivating this ability is to cultivate mindfulness (see Chapter 6: Strength Robbers, about how you might start to do this right now). It's about learning to notice our thoughts and feelings, but also the traps we fall into: our unhelpful patterns of thought. It's about experiencing these thoughts and feelings as they happen in the present moment. The other part of the Wake up! stage is what practitioners of ACT call 'self as context'. This basically means developing a perspective on our experience that's bigger than our actual experience, so that we are able to separate ourselves from our thoughts and observe ourselves as separate from them. If we can learn to do this, then we don't have to be defined by our thoughts and we begin to see ourselves as simply the context in which our thoughts happen, rather than *being* them. (See the box from Consultant

Counselling Psychologist Dr Michael Sinclair later on in this section.)

2. **Loosen up**

This stage is all about responding to your thoughts and feelings in a more effective way – a way that fosters resilience. Psychologists call the way we respond to our thoughts or feelings 'cognitive diffusion techniques', so Loosen up is all about developing good ones! Again, as we explored in earlier chapters, these would be first and foremost noticing and becoming aware of our thoughts (instead of just reacting to them). It also means not buying into negative thoughts such as: I'm useless/I can't do anything. 'These,' explains Dr Sinclair, are 'autopilot responses of distraction. They're like turning the TV up louder.'

If we buy into thoughts like this, it affects us behaviourally, and we might feel down and anxious; we might 'fuse' with this feeling, which is the word psychologists use to describe getting unhelpfully caught up with a feeling, often creating an unhelpful narrative around it.

The Loosen up stage also means not trying to suppress our feelings. To illustrate how unhelpful trying to deny our feelings is, try this: DON'T think about chocolate, what it tastes, looks, feels like … See? All you do is think about chocolate and how it tastes and what it looks like! Basically, the harder you try to throw something away, the harder it bounces back. Trying to suppress thoughts isn't helpful, instead cultivate the awareness to say 'this isn't working. I need to loosen up'.

The other piece in Loosen up is acceptance. It means developing your willingness to experience feelings without putting up defences. The more we do this, the more quickly we can move towards the things we want to do/should be doing and the quicker we can feel stronger and better in general.

3. **Step up**

   This stage is about clarifying our values. What do you want
   to stand for in this adversity? Who do you want to be and
   what qualities do you want to display and prove? We already
   looked at values and how to find yours in Chapter 4, but let's
   look deeper. Dr Michael Sinclair defines a value as a 'desired,
   ongoing, global quality of action'. Basically, values are not
   goals – they are the qualities we want to bring to the way in
   which we pursue and hopefully achieve our goals. Our values
   inform how we're going to do it, and why … For example, a goal
   might be: I want to get through this adversity; but the value
   might be: by being kinder to myself, by being a calmer mother
   while I do it. When we take the time and trouble to find out
   what really matters to us, then live our lives accordingly, we
   feel much stronger and self-confident. We have 'stepped up'.

4. **Committed action**

   This is the bit where you JUST DO IT! You put into practice the
   promises you made to yourself about living out your values and
   you start to actually make changes. One great way of doing
   this is goal setting. Goals give us hope, direction and focus.
   Setting them is about creating a vision, and having a vision is a
   big part of building real strength. It's about having the mindset:
   let's keep working towards the things I want to happen, *despite*
   the fact I'm going through adversity.

One tried and tested way of setting goals is what psychologists
call 'SMART'-based goal setting. The acronym SMART has several
slightly different variations, which can be used to provide a more
comprehensive definition of goal setting, but here is the one used
in ACT.

- **S:** Specific. Try and make your goals as defined as possible.
  So, rather than 'I want to lose weight', say 'I want to lose ten
  pounds'.

- **M:** Measurable. This is about being able to monitor your progress; so can you measure the weight you are now, and make a note of how much you lose every week? Or, to give a different example, can you measure how many jobs you've applied for this week, against how many jobs you intended to apply for (your goal) and work out how you will split up the remainder?

- **A:** Achievable. Know if the goal is obtainable and how far away completion is.

- **R:** Recorded/Realistic. Can you achieve this goal with the resources, knowledge and time you have?

- **T:** Time-based. What time frame do you want to achieve the goal within and is this enough time to complete it?

If we look back at the four different stages of ACT, then, we could breakdown and summarize the whole process like this:

1. Contact the present moment.
2. Hold onto those thoughts and feelings lightly and with self-compassion.
3. Observe those thoughts and feelings as they pass through you.
4. Clarify what actions you can take – and engage in those steps.

DR MICHAEL SINCLAIR ON HOW TO SEPARATE YOURSELF FROM YOUR THOUGHTS

- *'Imagine coming up against adversity like playing a game of chess: imagine the black and white pieces on the chessboard; the black pieces are negative thoughts and the white pieces are positive thoughts.*

- *We move a negative thought forward and put a positive thought in its place, but then a negative thought very soon replaces that and on it goes. If we're not careful, we get caught up in this battle between negative and positive thoughts: I'm useless, no I'm not! Come on! No, I'm useless … The battle is endless though, as there are an infinite number of black and white pieces, it goes round and round.*

- *So then imagine these pieces are your thoughts and YOU are the chess board. The board has endless room for the thoughts, but it's firm and stable and it doesn't get involved in the battle, it just allows those pieces to pass over it. This is a helpful way of looking at our thoughts. We are more expansive than them, they exist in the context of us. We are NOT our thoughts. By standing back from our thoughts and gaining perspective on them, we realize they're separate to us. We can immediately feel stronger: if our thoughts are the pieces, then the board is us, we can just let our thoughts glide over us.*

- *Sing or rap your thoughts out loud. Repeat then rapidly or really slowly. It will help to remind you that your thoughts are just a sound, produced by your mind!*

- *Repeating troublesome thoughts with a few words before them can also help you gain perspective on your thoughts, recognizing them for what they are – just thoughts. These few words are: "I am having the thought that …. [add your troublesome thought here]".*

- *Remember that whether a thought is true or not is not the point. It's more important to ask whether thinking a thought is helpful or not. For example, is thinking this thought helping you stay resilient? Is it moving you towards what you care about/want to be doing? Gaining perspective on your thoughts like this gives you an opportunity to consider how helpful it is to be thinking them, and then choose whether you want to continue to think them or not.'*

GROW SOME GRIT

In Chapter 3 we were introduced to author Angela Duckworth and the concept of 'grit'. We learned how, as part of her research, Duckworth interviewed and studied army cadets going through a grueling training programme. (For the record, she also studied children doing a spelling bee and trainee primary school teachers as they were thrown into the lion's den of an inner city state school.) We heard how she discovered that the one quality those who stayed the course, no matter how hard it was, had in common, was what she coined as 'grit': the ultimate blend of 'passion and perseverance'.

We can now see, then, the close correlation between grittiness and real strength: if we have passion and perseverance, we are much more likely to be able to stick at things when tackling a problem or challenge and to come out the other side, not crushed, but thriving.

> ❝ **Grit fails when we can't get back up after a setback, but when we do, it prevails.** ❞
>
> Angela Duckworth, author of *Grit*

The obvious question now is: if being gritty is such an essential part of thriving after adversity, can I develop it? Say you're not ordinarily the kind of person who sticks things out once the going gets tough, can you learn to be?

The answer to that is a resounding yes. Seeing as passion and perseverance are the two vital components of grit, it would follow that if we can learn how to develop each one, we can develop grit.

We already looked at how to find your passion and the goal hierarchy in Chapter 4, so let's look now at perseverance.

Perseverance and how to develop yours

In a nutshell, perseverance is the act of persisting to do something in spite of challenges, obstacles and disappointments. It is an essential quality, a type of real strength if you like, which is essential not just for grit but for realizing your goals in general.

Unfortunately, many people rob themselves of success because they do not have the perseverance to see their goals through. However, developing perseverance is not difficult to do if you're prepared to put in some effort. The following is a kind of checklist you can look to for helping you develop perseverance and become grittier!

- First, establish what it is you truly desire. What goal do you really want to achieve?

- You have to have an unshakeable faith and belief that you CAN overcome your adversity or achieve your goal, no matter what obstacles you come up against.

- If you don't, then the likelihood is that you'll quit, which only reinforces your theory that you wouldn't have ever succeeded anyway.

- If you're not careful, this mindset can develop into a habit, meaning you fall into the trap of sabotaging potential success.

- To help you with confidence, it's a great idea to have a clear step-by-step plan of how you're going to achieve your goal. Your plan is your roadmap – without one, you've far more chance of getting lost!

- Before you start your pursuit of a goal, make a commitment to yourself that you will work toward it for a specific period of time and won't give up before that time is up.

- When the deadline arrives, you can then decide whether to continue with the strategy you're currently following or make some changes to it.

- Be flexible. Have belief and willingness to revise your game-plan, because revising things is fine, but giving up will only reinforce your idea that you're unable to see things through and undermine your confidence.

- Identify potential obstacles you could face along the way. This will not only prepare you for when you do come across them, but it will also help you devise plan B/alternative strategies.

- Seek out support from family, friends or mentors to help keep you motivated.

- Remember: It's all about the baby steps. Establishing habits every day towards your main goal will mean that your efforts will accumulate.

BEYOND 'REAL STRENGTH' TO 'SUPER RESILIENCE'

In Chapter 5, you were introduced to psychologist Elizabeth Kubler-Ross' 'grief model' and the five cognitive stages of grief and loss; be this loss of a loved one, of self, or loss of your hopes and dreams.

Just to remind you of those five stages:

1. Denial.
2. Anger.
3. Bargaining.
4. Depression.
5. Acceptance.

This last stage – acceptance – is what we talk about when we talk about resilience or 'bouncing back'. If we think about the phrase itself – 'bouncing back' – we can see how it describes getting back to our lives after adversity: how we carry on, willing to live with, 'accepting' whatever loss or pain we've endured.

Motivational speaker and author Dr Gregg Steinberg, however, believes there is a final stage that we are capable of – a higher stage. This stage he calls transcendence:

> **"Transcendence is not just accepting the tragedy – not just bouncing back to the same spot – but bouncing back higher. It is being super-resilient."**
>
> Dr Gregg Steinberg, motivational speaker and author of *Fall Up!*

Eager to learn the 'secret of using adversity as a superpower for personal growth', Steinberg interviewed thousands of people around the world who declared that their tragic events had propelled their life to a higher level of existence, meaning they discovered not just their true path in life, but also joy they could never have imagined.

The result is his book: *Fall Up! Why Adversity Unlocks your Superpowers.* It is a book that shares these stories, but also Steinberg's discovery that in their journey from tragedy to transcendence, every single person he interviewed went through the same steps in the same order. Just as Kubler-Ross called the five stages of grief she discovered the 'grief cycle model', Steinberg called these stages 'The Science of Transcendability'.

'These people used adversity as a super-power for personal growth', says Steinberg.

Here, he tells us how it's done.

DR GREGG STEINBERG ON HOW TO 'FALL UP!'

'Stage 1: The wake-up call

At this stage, the adversity awakens you to the realization that you are not on your true path. Some people have described this as if they were sleepwalking through life and the hardship awakened them from their slumber.

Stage 2: Flip the switch

Here, you make the shift to believe the event has a purposeful connection in your life. This tragic event sparks the realization that you must redesign your life for the better.

Stage 3: Release your genius

When you move into this new direction, you are forced out of your comfort zone. This process helps you to see talents that you never knew existed – for example, writing, setting up a charity, running marathons. You then use these newfound strengths to move to the next step.

Stage 4: Create your LIFESONG

At this stage, all the distractions, chaos, and misinformation that have pervaded your life during your period of adversity quieten down. Now, you can finally hear your true lifesong – your life's purpose. Because of this, you live in your flow and find joy and contentment beyond compare.

Stage 5: You begin to live in the 'we' spot

At this final stage, you move from a 'me' mentality to a 'we' mentality. You let go of the ego and stop being so selfish. Because your focus is to have a meaningful impact in the world, you radiate amazing energy and the world responds in kind. This is the sweet spot in life.'

Each of these stages gives you a map for bouncing back higher and becoming the person you're meant to be. Also, you don't need to have experienced serious tragedy to want to, or know how to, transcend. Maybe you are just stuck in a rut or unhappy with your life, but feel you're on the threshold of that wake-up call to have the life you always wanted to have, and be the person you wanted to be.

We hope this chapter has been useful and, above all, inspiring. Take some time to read and absorb the information, then make it work for you. Perhaps you're still finding your way through the mire of whatever trauma you've been through – or are currently going through – and aren't yet ready to think about bouncing back, never mind, bouncing back higher! And that's fine. Whether it's trying to simply work on your perseverance or listening to your newfound calling and setting up a charity – going at your pace is not just an important part, but a vital part, of building real strength. Good luck!

ASK YOURSELF

Q Have you had the 'wake-up call'? In other words, do you feel the urge and motivation to change your life?

Q What one thing could you do, that is outside your comfort zone, to do that? To shake up your life in a big way?

Q Could it be something that benefits not just yourself, but other people?

Q If you had to say what your 'calling' has always been (whether you have reached it yet or not), what would it be?

REAL PEOPLE

"Treatment for cancer made me a stronger person physically and mentally." *– Judy*

Judy Lewis on how her life changed for the better after surgery for cancer of the jaw.

'I'd been generally poorly since the beginning of 2009. I developed a terrible pain that went from my left temple to my lower jaw. I had a full-time job and a two-year old son – I couldn't afford to get seriously ill. Eventually, my dentist referred me to a maxilliofacial unit and, in October 2009, I was diagnosed with spindle cell sarcoma of the lower jaw – a very rare type of bone cancer.

It was to be chemo and surgery all within a month, since the tumour was quite advanced. Surgery would mean removing the diseased part of my jaw and rebuilding it with bone from my fibula (the thin bone that runs parallel to the shin bone). It would never look the same again. The worst part, however, was that the chemotherapy would make me infertile, and I really wanted to have more children. I was rushed in for IVF – it was our one window of opportunity. Two months later, I was menopausal.

So I was dealing with a cancer diagnosis, the prospect of severe scarring to my face and legs and the fact I'd never have more children. It was horrendous, but in a way, the diagnosis was a relief. At least now, we knew what it was, and I thought: I can do this. I never thought for a moment that I wouldn't make it. Chemotherapy was grueling but life had to carry on as normal because of Woody – my son. My main concern now, however, was: how do you prepare your two-year old for looking different?

Interestingly, he didn't think I *did*! It was me who howled the first time I saw my new face. I couldn't recognize myself, I didn't look like a woman: my face was so swollen, I had no bottom teeth, then there was the task of learning to walk, talk and eat again. But although this was the lowest physically I'd ever been, the emotional nosedive didn't come until after I'd received the all clear. I was utterly spent and depressed, but one day, one of the nurses from my team came to see me. She said: 'Look, you should be proud of your scars – they're the reason you're alive.' That changed everything for me.

I felt ready for the emotional fight now. I contacted the charity Changing Faces. They help people with visible and non-visible differences. I had some one-to-one counseling sessions with them. With their gentle guidance and support, I quite quickly got my mojo back. I became what's called a 'buddy' to other patients going through the same thing and also started doing some voluntary work with Changing Faces. The time I spend with patients has enriched my life no end. For them to see me and think – she did it, so can I – is one of the greatest feelings in the world. To see them walk a little taller, to help them empower themselves.

Once I'd recovered, I also took up long-distance running and I've now completed three half-marathons and two full ones, raising money for Changing Faces and the Head and Neck department at University College hospital and the reconstructive surgery unit at the Royal Free.

When training is tough, I think to myself, compared to what I've been through, this is a walk in the park. It's given me so much mental and physical strength and if I can inspire just one patient with my story of how I went from 'she'll never walk again' to running marathons, I'll be happy!

So much good has come out of what I've been through. I like to think I'm a more compassionate person and I have learnt how to dig deep when the going gets tough, with what reserves I have. I know no matter how bad things get, I can cope.

For me, resilience is being able to step back so that you are in the moment. It's about having the mental strength to not cave and the belief that even if you don't know what to do right now, if you can just hold on until you get that information, or find someone who can help, you can do it. You have to be flexible too and trust those around you. Most of all, you have to believe in yourself'.

WHAT NEXT?

We hope that you are feeling more confident and optimistic about not only your ability to get through adversity but also, most importantly, to grow from it. Maybe you have discovered reserves of strength you never knew you had. Or perhaps you feel (we certainly hope so!) that you have already grown as a person. If you thought that real strength was something you either had or didn't have, rather than something you could cultivate and learn, we hope we've challenged that idea. Because our philosophy is that anyone can become more resilient and everyone has reserves of strength – it's just knowing how to tap into them. We hope this book helps you to do that.

We're not saying that adversity – in whatever form you experience it – is not difficult. When we're knee-deep in the middle of it, it can feel like there is nothing good to be gained from it. But we hope we've demonstrated that we all *need* it. Quite simply, without upheaval and struggle, we can't grow and learn; we can't not just survive but thrive. As the saying goes, however, it's not what happens to you, it's how you deal with it that counts. We hope that by now you have picked up some new strategies and tips to do just that – and well.

What next? You'll be working on really getting to know yourself better in order to work out what your strengths, weak spots and triggers are. You'll feel more confident about your ability to get curious about your emotions and be willing to feel them, rather than to fight them. We've given you plenty of tips and the latest tried and tested strategies from experts in resilience to do just that. With the 'Ask Yourself' questions, you'll also be able to explore what's really stopping you from feeling strong and how you can tap into and grow the strength we know you already have.

Above all, we hope that you feel generally more optimistic in your ability to overcome this period in your life. We hope that even if you can't yet see the light at the end of the tunnel, you know there's one waiting for you, when you're ready. The real strength you have gained by reading this book will help you to get there. And waiting for you will be greater contentment, but also the knowledge that when the next bad patch comes along, you are as equipped as possible to deal with it. Because this is what real strength is about after all, not just the ability to deal with one setback, but the many setbacks we will all experience in life. Every human being on the planet gets thrown lemons now and again, all that's left for you to do now – with everything you have learned – is to turn those into sweet lemonade! Good luck.

ABOUT PSYCHOLOGIES

MAGAZINE

Psychologies is a magazine read by those who want to lead a fulfilling life, who want to live a life on their own terms, however you choose to define it. *Psychologies* helps you discover what 'life success' looks like for you – from the inside out.

We're on a mission to find out from the best experts and latest research in psychology how we can all lead happier and more fulfilling lives. *Psychologies* is not about striving to do more but rather finding ways to BE more. Who are you? And what do you really want? These are questions we're always asking ourselves. *Psychologies* magazine is about being the best you, and we mean being in an active way: becoming the best you can be, the happiest and the most fulfilled you.

We focus on helping you understand yourself and the world around you, by gathering the latest, most compelling thinking and translating it into practical wisdom that can support you as you create the life that works for you.

Real Strength is written by journalist and novelist, Katy Regan. After ten years as staff writer and columnist on various women's magazines, Katy became Commissioning Editor of *Marie-Claire* magazine. In 2008, she left the world of magazines to write novels. She has, to date, published four novels – the latest being *The Story of You*. Her fifth novel, *Little Big Man*, will be published by Mantle (Pan Macmillan) in October. She was the author of *Real Focus*, the second in the *Psychologies* series. Visit her author website at www.katyregan.com and follow her on Twitter @katyreganwrites. Katy lives in Hertfordshire with her son.

Notes